What is the History of Emotions?

What is History? series

John H. Arnold, *What is Medieval History?*

Peter Burke, *What is Cultural History?* 2nd edition

Peter Burke, *What is the History of Knowledge?*

John C. Burnham, *What is Medical History?*

Pamela Kyle Crossley, *What is Global History?*

Pero Gaglo Dagbovie, *What is African American History?*

Shane Ewen, *What is Urban History?*

Christiane Harzig and Dirk Hoerder, with Donna Gabaccia, *What is Migration History?*

J. Donald Hughes, *What is Environmental History?* 2nd edition

Andrew Leach, *What is Architectural History?*

Stephen Morillo with Michael F. Pavkovic, *What is Military History?* 3rd edition

James Raven, *What is the History of the Book?*

Sonya O. Rose, *What is Gender History?*

Brenda E. Stevenson, *What is Slavery?*

Jeffrey Weeks, *What is Sexual History?*

Richard Whatmore, *What is Intellectual History?*

What is the History of Emotions?

Barbara H. Rosenwein
and Riccardo Cristiani

polity

First published in 2018 by Polity Press

Reprinted 2019 (three times), 2021, 2022

Polity Press
65 Bridge Street
Cambridge CB2 1UR, UK

Polity Press
101 Station Landing
Suite 300
Medford, MA 02155, USA

ISBN-13: 978-1-5095-0849-5 (hardback)
ISBN-13: 978-1-5095-0850-1 (paperback)

A catalogue record for this book is available from the British Library.

Typeset in 10.5 on 12 pt Sabon by Toppan Best-set Premedia Limited
Printed and bound in the UK by CPI Group (UK) Ltd, Croydon, CR0 4YY

The publisher has used its best endeavors to ensure that the URLs for external websites referred to in this book are correct and active at the time of going to press. However, the publisher has no responsibility for the websites and can make no guarantee that a site will remain live or that the content is or will remain appropriate.

For further information on Polity, visit our website: politybooks.com

For Joshua and Julian
In ricordo di Chiara Zevi

Contents

Preface and Acknowledgments

We began to think about writing this book while working on *Generations of Feeling* together. Although the history of emotions has flourished in the last several decades, it is open to a wide variety of assumptions, expectations, and approaches. In many ways, it is still finding itself. We hope that this book will make following its many paths a bit easier. Writing it certainly helped us to see many unexpected coherencies and patterns.

While preparing this book, we have incurred many debts. We warmly thank Damien Boquet, Lynn Hunt, and Jan Plamper, whose comments and critiques on earlier drafts gave us welcome advice. Lale Behzadi, Maaike van Berkel, Anthony Cardoza, Nicole Eustace, Timothy Gilfoyle, and Kyle Roberts helped with important sections. We are grateful to Fay Bound Alberti, Paolo Arcangeli, James Averill, Thomas Dixon, John Donoghue, Stephanie Downes, Ute Frevert, Erik Goosmann, Bernard Rimé, Lyndal Roper, and Tom Rosenwein. A teaching engagement at the University of Reykjavik allowed Barbara to try out some of the materials that are discussed in Chapters 1 and 2. She thanks the participants and organizers, especially Torfi H. Tulinius and Sigurður Gylfi Magnússon. Finally, we thank our editor at Polity Press, Pascal Porcheron, and the Press's anonymous readers, who commented with care and intelligence on an earlier draft.

Barbara H. Rosenwein and
Riccardo Cristiani
Sanremo, March 2017

Introduction

"Is it really possible to tell someone else what one feels?"

Leo Tolstoy, *Anna Karenina*

"I understand a fury in your words. But not your words."

William Shakespeare, *Othello*, Act 4, Scene 2

When Othello walks into his wife's bedroom, it is the way that he speaks, not his words, that she understands. "Let me see your eyes," he says. "Look in my face." Spoken tenderly, these could have been a lover's request. Desdemona knows better. She understands that behind them is a "fury," though she does not grasp its source. Othello begins to cry. "Alas the heavy day, why do you weep?" asks his wife.

These are the words of characters in a play written some four hundred years ago. They tell us some of the complex ways in which Shakespeare understood emotions and their expression. That we can still be moved by this scene means that we can be sympathetic to the emotional burdens of its protagonists. But are they our emotional burdens? And would we express them the same way? The history of emotions is dedicated to answering such questions. It studies the emotions that were felt and expressed in the past; it looks at what has changed and what ties together their past and present.

In the last twenty-five years or so, emotions have become a kind of obsession in our culture. Now everyone – novelists, journalists, psychologists, neuropsychologists, philosophers, and sociologists – thinks and writes about emotions, each for his or her own purposes, each taking a different direction. Historians are no exception. While united in the goal of understanding the past of emotions, they have pursued it in a bewildering variety of ways. Anyone interested in the history of emotions – whether student, researcher, or simply curious reader – will find the terrain difficult without a map. That is what this book provides. It introduces the main avenues of modern research on emotions, starting with the psychological sciences, continuing with the various "schools" of historical thought on the topic, adding trends in current studies, and ending with a glimpse of the future. Much like a Google map, it suggests a variety of possible approaches so that readers may pursue their own historical inquiries. It is not the first book to survey the field, but it is the first to do so as both a short introduction and a guide to fledgling researchers.[1]

The history of emotions relies on some sort of conception of what an emotion is. This is more problematic than it seems at first glance. How do we know – ironic as it may seem – that an emotion *is* an emotion? We know (or think we know) the answer. "How do you feel about that?" ask our relatives, spouses, friends, our therapist, or a TV reporter. "Happy," or "angry", we say, or we burst into tears, or our hearts beat faster. But how exactly are those words, tears, and beating hearts signs of emotions, or emotions themselves? What makes those words, gestures, and the concepts they embrace "emotions"? Are we born with them? Or do we learn them? Are they rational or irrational? Do we really know how we feel, or might it be better to say that emotions involve something beyond our knowledge?

These questions have occupied philosophers, physicians, and theologians for centuries and are now largely the province of scientists, sociologists, and anthropologists. Historians, too, have much to say. They know that past societies defined emotions in ways that may seem odd today. They know that the word "emotion" itself is slippery: even Western societies once used words like passions, affects, affections, sentiments, but had no word "emotion" as such. Indeed, the term is of fairly recent vintage, though "motion" and "movement" were often used in ages past. Historians also know that – whatever the term – these things that we today call emotions have been defined differently at different times. The Romans thought that "benevolence" was an emotion, and the medieval scholastic Thomas Aquinas said the same of "weariness." Few people today would agree.

Not that people today are of the same mind about what emotions are. In fact, there is considerable debate about how to define them, and the differences exist not only among disciplines but also within each of them. In this book, the scientific definitions – and they alone are legion – are the focus of Chapter 1. We begin with early definitions and modern disagreements, followed by discussions of the theories of two of the chief pioneers in the science of emotions, Darwin and James, and their modern heirs. While these theories tended to emphasize the body, the 1960s saw the development of cognitivist theories and, shortly thereafter, social constructionist discussions, both of which focused on the mind. Neuroscientists represent the most recent scientific developments; nevertheless, they generally work within one of these traditions and are therefore just as varied in their approaches.[2]

In Chapter 2 we begin our discussion of histories of emotions. Our emphasis here and throughout the book is on methods. We present the major questions and approaches that historians of emotions employ. If our examples of their results come largely from Western history, that is in part because much of the work on the topic has been Western in focus, and in part because that is the field most familiar to the authors of this book. But the methods themselves cut across all periods, fields, and continents.

After glancing at the "prehistory" of emotions historiography, Chapter 2 turns to the foundational work of Peter Stearns and his then-wife Carol Stearns, whose notion of "emotionology" was elaborated in the 1980s. Drawing on social constructionism, they separated "how people really felt" from "standards of emotional expression." They looked at, for example, advice books that prescribed how and when to get angry or how to control anger – without worrying about whether people really "felt" angry. Standards changed over time, and thus (observed the Stearnses) a history of emotions was possible. Meanwhile, in the 1990s and early 2000s, William M. Reddy introduced the twin concepts of "emotional regimes" and "emotives" to make emotions the key to power and power the key to emotions. Emotional regimes, too, changed over time, particularly when they stifled emotional experimentation. Less all-encompassing and more varied than Reddy's emotional regimes were the "emotional communities" proposed – around the same time – by Barbara H. Rosenwein, one of the authors of this book. Emotional communities were (and are) groups of people who share the same or similar valuations of particular emotions, goals, and norms of emotional expression. In Rosenwein's view, the very variety of these communities were themselves agents of change as they interacted with one another and responded to changing circumstances. For various reasons and in a variety of ways, Stearns', Reddy's, and Rosenwein's approaches have all been cited and used by subsequent historians. While different, their theories have one important commonality: their emphasis is on texts and words. This is less true of the final foundational approach discussed in Chapter 2, that of Gerd Althoff and the notion of emotions as "performances." Although dependent on texts for descriptions of such performances, Althoff stressed the emotional gestures of the ruler's body to communicate his will to his subjects.

How do these different historical approaches work in concrete cases? We have chosen the Declaration of Independence of the United States to illustrate the four "in action." The Declaration is obviously famous if less evidently emotional. And yet, its repeated grievances suggest emotional gestures, and the one mention of "happiness" – whose pursuit is proclaimed a universal and inalienable right – poses instant, ineluctable questions to the historian of emotions.

At its core, "happiness" is just a word. Recently, many historians have become dissatisfied with the limits imposed by words and texts. After examining major current trends in such emotions studies, we came to realize that their common theme was the body, though defined in two main ways. In one, the body is bounded and autonomous. In the other, it is porous, open to – and even merging with – the world. Chapter 3 begins with the bounded body. Its many organs have at one time or another been associated with emotions; its flesh and viscera subject to pain. Gender, too, was originally tied to sex organs, but more recently has been seen as a sort of "performance." Elaborating on that approach,

some historians propose that emotions are the habitual practices of the body, which both create and reinforce emotional
experience.

We continue Chapter 3 with the "porous" body. This is
a body that spills into the world and absorbs it in turn. We
explore how some historians speak of affects – "emotions"
that, by this view, are totally or largely unconscious, divorced
from intention and verbal articulation – as they move out
from and into the body. We look at how the body interacts
with space, moving within it and endowing it with emotional
meaning even as it affects people in turn. We then turn to
the body's porous relations with matter. In the most recent
developments in this line of inquiry, anthropologists, sociologists, and historians have thought about the "social life of
things." Even ordinary objects – such as clothes, heirlooms,
and household furnishings – influence or change our feelings
and contribute to shaping our needs and values, just as we
shape matter itself. Until recently, for example, Shakespeare's
famous bequest of his "second best bed" to his wife was
considered evidence of his indifference toward her. But now,
thanks to new technical analyses of his will, a British team
argues that Shakespeare inserted that clause after the others,
at a time when he was severely ill. His second-best bed was
thus one among the "tokens of affection from a man facing
the prospect of his death."[3] The chapter ends with a discussion of mental space, which incorporates matter and place
by way of memory, dreams, and imagination.

These chapters explore exciting frontiers. But they also
raise questions about where the history of emotions is – and
should be – going. In Chapter 4 we look at the place of the
history of emotions in today's world and what it could be in
the future. We consider its untapped potential to partner with
the science of emotions and with inquiries in other fields, and
we probe its implications for historical thought. We look at
its significant achievements and challenges within academia.
Convinced that the history of emotions is more than simply
an "academic exercise," we seek a future for it outside the
classroom, where we think it could (and should) diffuse its
lessons more widely. Here we consider, by way of example,
two influential products of today's culture: children's books
and videogames. Our brief Conclusion takes up some of the

objections that have been made about the field and ends with what we consider to be its major successes.

Though perhaps with less deadly consequences, Desdemona's dilemma is nonetheless our own. We have a sense of our feelings and those of other people, but they are hard to fathom fully. Today scientists have some solutions to offer us. Historians have others, and this book is an introduction to what they teach.

1
Science

"When I use a word," Humpty Dumpty said in rather a scornful tone, "it means just what I choose it to mean – neither more nor less." "The question is," said Alice, "whether you can make words mean so many different things." "The question is," said Humpty Dumpty, "which is to be master – that's all."

Lewis Carroll, *Through the Looking Glass*

Political history is about power relations: kings, queens, revolutions, constitutions, and the like. Military history is about war: campaigns, arms, battles, and so on. We have fairly clear notions of these topics. But what is the history of emotions about? How can we have a history of something unless we have a definition of it first? What are emotions?

Premodern views

Although the category "emotion" is itself relatively new, nearly equivalent terms – such as motions, affections, and passions – were part of the languages of the West from the time of the ancient Greeks. The semantic fields of these terms were (and are) not precisely coterminous, and, furthermore, even the modern English word "emotions" means different things to different researchers. Nonetheless, the commonalities are enough to allow for discussion, as long as we recognize the fuzziness of the terms.[1]

Theorizing the emotions was long the preserve of philosophers. Aristotle (d.322 BCE) devoted many pages to the topic
in the second book of his *Art of Rhetoric*. The orator had
to sway his audience, and that was a matter not only of
setting forth facts, but also of moving hearts. The emotions,
said Aristotle (using the ancient Greek term *pathe*), "are all
those affections which cause men to change their opinion in
regard to their judgments, and are accompanied by pleasure
and pain; such are anger, pity, fear, and all similar emotions
and their contraries." For Aristotle, emotions were forms of
cognition: they depended on the individual's assessment of any
given situation. Consider the case of anger, which interested
Aristotle (and other ancient philosophers) very much. It was
evoked by "a real or apparent slight, affecting a man himself
or one of his friends, when such a slight is undeserved." This
definition relied on cognition: it meant that a person judged
not only that someone had slighted him (or her) but also that
the slight was undeserved.[2]

Later, in the Hellenistic period (323 to 31 BCE), Stoic and
Epicurean philosophers made the study of emotions a specialty,
but only to master and overcome them. For the Stoics, emotions consisted in two sequential judgments: first the appraisal
that something – whether internal or external – was good or
bad; second the decision about how to react. On the whole,
they considered all emotional reactions to be wrong-headed.
There was no way to avoid the first inklings of emotion – a
sinking feeling, a blush, chattering teeth – but the wise person
refused to assent to them, refused to allow those so-called
"first movements" to become true emotions. "That anger
is stimulated by the impression of injury received is not in
doubt; what we are asking is whether it follows immediately
upon the impression itself ... or whether it is generated when
the mind assents." So wrote the Roman philosopher Seneca
(d.65 CE), for whom assent was the crucial factor.[3]

With the conversion of the Roman Empire to Christianity
at the end of the fourth century, theologians rather than philosophers became the chief theorists of the emotions. Many
early Christian ascetics accepted the Stoics' wary view, but
others welcomed emotions – as long as they were directed
in the correct way, toward God and not toward things of
this world. Augustine of Hippo (d.430) set the terms of the

discussion: "The character of a man's will is at issue. For if it is turned the wrong way [away] from God], it will turn these emotions awry; but if it is straight, they will be not only blameless, but even praiseworthy."[4]

As theology merged with philosophy and medicine in the thirteenth century, ever more complex discussions of the emotions ensued. In the seventeenth century, philosopher and mathematician René Descartes's treatise on *The Passions of the Soul* (1649) seemed to separate mind and body, a dualism that would later have long-term repercussions. Philosopher and physician John Locke's *An Essay Concerning Human Understanding* (1690) made the passions, from love to shame, the product of experience. Well into the eighteenth century, theologians, physicians, and philosophers continued to share the task of theorizing the emotions. But over time, secular, mechanistic, and physicalist approaches came to dominate. During the nineteenth century, "emotions" became the term of choice, displacing passions, affections, and many other words. As a convenient and simple category ripe for investigation, that term set the stage for the present near-monopoly by experimental scientists. To be sure, sociologists and anthropologists have much to say on the topic, and we shall bring them into the discussion from time to time. But at the forefront of the public eye today are the scientists. The remainder of this chapter will explore their chief theories, for historians of the modern field of the history of emotions cannot – and usually do not wish to – escape them.[5]

The science of emotions

In 1981, psychologist Paul R. Kleinginna and Anne M. Kleinginna, dismayed by the bewildering proliferation of definitions of emotions that had been proposed by their peers, tried to find common ground. Surveying the field, they found ninety-two different answers and nine "skeptical statements." Working with them all, they came up with a hybrid definition on which, they hoped, everyone would agree:

> Emotion is a complex set of interactions among subjective and objective factors, mediated by neural/hormonal systems, which can (a)

give rise to affective experiences such as feelings of arousal, pleasure/
displeasure; (b) generate cognitive processes such as emotionally
relevant perceptual effects, appraisals, labeling processes; (c) activate
widespread physiological adjustments to the arousing conditions;
and (d) lead to behavior that is often, but not always, expressive,
goal-directed, and adaptive.[6]

Although cited every so often, this definition is hardly ever
adopted, no doubt because by trying to please all, it pleases
none.

More helpful is a textbook from 1996 by psychologist
Randolf Cornelius, *The Science of Emotion*. Cornelius covered
four foundational theories of modern psychology: the Darwinian, Jamesian, cognitivist, and social constructionist. We
will review them in this chapter, for they continue to be the
paradigms that scientists work with today, and we will show
along the way how they manifest themselves in the newest
trend in the science of emotions: neuropsychology. In Chapter
4, we will see how they turn up in our children's books and
in videogames, for this provides a glimpse of the pervasive-
ness of these theories not just in textbooks but also in lived
experience – including the lived experience of historians.

There is also Freudian, or psychoanalytic, theory. It is
of particular importance for therapy and for inquiries into
the unconscious, but does not lend itself well to the experimental method favored by most scientists. Psychoanalysis
was influential in "psychohistory," which flourished in the
1970s. Although certainly touching on emotions, neither psychoanalysis nor psychohistory focused on that topic, being
concerned, rather, with drives (the so-called sex and death
instincts) and their role in the formation and functions of the
id, ego, and super-ego in individual development and human
relationships.[7]

Are they emotions or are they not? Moods, feelings, sentiments, affects

When Cornelius began his book on the science of emotions,
he presented some examples rather than give an abstract
definition: "This is a book about emotions. It is about joy,
love, anger, fear, happiness, guilt, sadness, embarrassment,

hope, and many other emotions as well."[8] Most of us and certainly most scientists agree that anger is an emotion. But is "depression" an emotion? Are feelings the same as emotions? When we say: I am "feeling sad," no doubt we mean to express an emotion. But when we say, "You hurt my feelings," no emotion per se has been hurt. To some degree historians of emotions do not need to worry too much about these fine distinctions, first because they were not necessarily made in the past (they are anachronistic) and second because historians must deal with complex phenomena that few in the past neatly labelled "an emotion."

However, the word "affect" poses a somewhat different problem. Used as the equivalent of emotion by many scholars, both in history and science, it also has been made the crux of a theory that deliberately separates affect from theories of emotions. This is a modern development. Derived from the Latin *affectus*, affect was traditionally used either as a word *for* the emotions or as one *of* the emotions. In the fifth century, Augustine used it interchangeably with other words for emotions – the Latin equivalents of words like perturbations, affections (a word with the same root as affect), motions of the soul, and passions. All of these, said Augustine, were in the will – a faculty of the soul (or mind). All emotions were good when turned towards God and bad if directed at worldly things. In the twelfth century, however, affect (and related words, like affections) tended to be linked specifically to love. Officials at the court of the counts of Toulouse used *affectuosus* (an adjective meaning "full of affect") to signify "affectionate." Around the same time, the monk and abbot Aelred of Rievaulx defined *affectus* as a spontaneous inclination of one person for another. In general, it was the irrational energy that gave love its force, whether for good or ill.[9]

That element of irrationality is the characteristic seized upon by affect theorists today. As theories of emotions emphasize ever more strongly the "cognitive" nature of emotions, affect theorists have allotted to affects the realm of the irrational. They are, according to these scholars, the pre-conscious, pre-emotional, pre-verbal forces in our lives. We will return to them when we come to the critics of cognitivist theory.

Charles Darwin: emotions as habits

Charles Darwin (d.1882) was the first modern scientist of emotions, and, in modified form, his theory remains the most influential of all among scientists today. When lay people think about emotions, they usually think first of subjective *feeling*. Darwin, by contrast, was interested in the physical "expression" of emotions. Moreover, he doubted that these expressions had any function in contemporary human life. They had originated for the purposes of survival, and they persisted out of inherited habits. Why do eyes open wide with surprise? Here is Darwin's answer: "We naturally desire, when startled, to perceive the cause as quickly as possible; and we consequently open our eyes fully, so that the field of vision may be increased."[10] The same gesture serves no purpose at, say, a surprise birthday party today. Even so, we open wide our eyes because it is a "built in" habit.

As the example of surprise demonstrates, Darwin thought that emotions were often expressed on faces. He was delighted by the photographs of "human emotions" that Duchenne de Boulogne published in 1862.[11] Duchenne electrically stimulated the facial muscles of people who suffered from facial nerve block, inducing in them the "look" of various emotional expressions. He then photographed the faces. Although such expressions could not possibly have represented the feelings of the people pictured (who, after all, were passively undergoing electrical stimulation), both Duchenne and Darwin considered the photographs to represent authentic emotions (see Plate 1).

Darwin's theory endured through the first half of the twentieth century and gained new momentum in the 1970s, above all with the work of Paul Ekman. In a famous study, Ekman and his collaborator, Wallace Friesen, claimed to show that six facial expressions of emotions – anger, disgust, fear, happiness, sadness, and surprise – were universal. That is because the faces were "correctly" identified not only by Westerners but also by members of the Fore tribal group in New Guinea. Ekman and Friesen (or rather their native translators) described a scenario to their Fore subjects – e.g. "His (her) friends have come, and he (she) is happy" – and then showed one "correct" photograph along with one or two "incorrect" photos of facial expressions corresponding to a selection among the six. The ratio of subjects choosing correct labels ranged from 100 percent (when the happiness face was shown alongside the disgust and anger faces) to 28 percent (when the fear face was paired with surprise and sadness). Today, the six, together with the later addition of "contempt," are often considered "basic" emotions.[12]

Ekman and his adherents do not deny that some cultures use rather different facial expressions than those in his photographs. But they argue that those differences are explained by superficial "display rules." The "real" emotions, nevertheless, manifest themselves in very brief "micro expressions."[13]

Ekman's work has been roundly criticized by scholars in a variety of disciplines. Anthropologist E. Richard Sorenson was present at Ekman's initial interactions with his Fore subjects. He was not impressed with the test protocol, noting that the translators probably influenced some responses. When he himself showed Ekman's photographs to the same Fore respondents, but did not accompany the pictures with stories, "many displayed uncertainty, hesitation and confusion. Some were completely tongue-tied; others trembled." Psychologist James A. Russell noted that the stories may well have signaled to the Fore that the faces were meant to respond to situations, not emotions. Further, he pointed out that the faces in Ekman's photographs – much like Duchenne's – were posed rather than spontaneous: how, then, did they show "real" emotions? Historian Ruth Leys analyzed Ekman's work in the context of the scientific issues and assumptions of the 1960s and beyond, noting that there were many dissenting voices from the start, and arguing that his work remains attractive largely because it avoids any discussion of human intention, a theme that requires deep contextual analysis. In this connection, Leys also remarks on "the convenience of Ekman's methods in facilitating research." Even his critics use his photographs.[14]

Indeed, a great many experiments by psychologists of every sort today use sets of posed photographs of faces that are meant to represent the basic emotions. Neuropsychologists sometimes use these faces together with fMRI studies (functional Magnetic Resonance Imaging) to discuss "emotion processing." The fMRI scans oxygen levels in the brain, and greater oxygenation signifies enhanced stimulation. In published experimental results, highly oxygenated brain regions are typically shown in color. Thus, for example, Taylor Keding and Ryan Herringa compared brain scans of non-traumatized healthy youths with those suffering from post-traumatic stress disorder (PTSD) as their subjects viewed "neutral" faces changing to "angry" or "happy." The researchers, looking at scans of the brain areas known as the amygdala/hippocampus and the medial prefrontal cortex as well as the whole brain, concluded that "PTSD youth showed reduced connectivity to angry faces, but increased connectivity to happy faces." In short, their findings suggested that youth with PTSD had to recruit more mental resources than other young people to process happy faces.[15]

Similarly, a study by neuropsychologist Sebastian Jongen and his colleagues undertook to locate the brain areas involved in incorrect "facial emotion recognition" in people who regularly misjudged such cues. (This disability is called alexithymia). The researchers used a FEEL (Facially Expressed Emotion Labeling) test based on the photographs developed by Ekman and his associates. They asked their subjects (some with alexithymia and others without) to name the emotions in forty-eight photographs, each displayed for two seconds on a computer screen. They found that people with a high degree of alexithymia did not recruit the same brain regions as others did when they attempted to recognize an emotional face. As this experiment suggests, psychologists in the Darwinian mold today do not think that emotions are just hold-overs from a more primitive past; they consider emotions to have real and important social functions even in the modern world. That is why people with alexithymia are considered abnormal rather than ultra-civilized.[16]

William James: emotions as bodily symptoms

When William James (d.1910) took up the topic of emotions not long after Darwin, he, too, was convinced that they were seated in the body. But he was interested in how bodies – not so much faces as changes in the internal organs – experienced emotions even before the person had a way to express them with his or her face or could find a word to describe them. Thus, James claimed that,

> If we fancy some strong emotion, and then try to abstract from our consciousness of it all the feelings of its characteristic bodily symptoms, we find we have nothing left behind, no "mind-stuff" out of which the emotion can be constituted, and that a cold and neutral state of intellectual perception is all that remains. ... What kind of an emotion of fear would be left, if the feelings neither of quickened heart-beats nor of shallow breathing, neither of trembling lips nor of weakened limbs, neither of goose-flesh nor of visceral stirrings, were present, it is quite impossible to think.

Like Darwin, James thought that these bodily changes were automatic. Excited by some perception, *"the bodily changes follow directly ... and our feeling of the same changes as they occur is the emotion."* It follows that "we feel sorry because we cry, angry because we strike, afraid because we tremble." The names that we give these feelings – sorrow, anger, fear – are by themselves "pale, colorless, destitute of emotional warmth." Only the body really knows the emotion.[17]

Moreover, the body feels each emotion in a particular and characteristic way. There are many possibilities and combinations of heartbeats, pulse, stomach and gut, breathing, muscle movements. As James put it: "the various permutations and combinations of which these organic activities are susceptible, make it abstractly possible that no shade of emotion, however slight, should be without a bodily reverberation as unique, when taken in its totality, as is the mental mood itself." James's emphasis, however, was on the many shades of bodily feeling rather than on finding absolute correlations between this or that bodily transformation and this or that emotion, since "every one of us, almost, has some personal idiosyncrasy of expression, laughing or sobbing differently from his neighbor." Nevertheless, he conjectured that if we mobilized all the physiological symptoms of an emotion, we would feel the emotion itself. Since so few of the bodily components of emotion could in fact be manipulated voluntarily, however, James doubted that this claim could be verified experimentally.[18]

James's theory, soon joined by the similar one of Carl Lange (d.1900), and now often called the James–Lange theory, had a more fluctuating career than Darwin's. Largely rejected in the 1930s, it has recently made a comeback. Psychologists today who find that bodily changes induce particular emotions are working within the Jamesian tradition. They often speak of "bodily feedback": what we do with our body produces our emotions. Much of the research for this shows how, for example, posing with a happy face makes us feel happy. More recently, neuroscientists have joined the discussion, arguing, as Antonio Damasio does, for example, that "actions ... ranging from facial and postural expressions to complex behaviors" produce internal responses that are represented in various regions of the brain "in distinctive patterns."[19]

The cognitivist view: thinking as emotion

When Aristotle and other ancient philosophers talked about emotions, they emphasized human judgment, not human bodies. Starting in the 1960s, psychologists revived this position, defining emotions as a certain kind of appraisal. "To arouse an emotion, the object must be appraised as affecting me in some way, affecting me personally as an individual with my particular experience and my particular aims." In this view, emotions are above all processes. They begin with an appraisal but go on to produce actions, physiological responses, and subjective feelings. These loop back on each other, so that all – including the initial appraisal itself – are constantly working on and modifying one another.[20]

Appraisals are not necessarily "cognitive" in the sense of conforming to reason or depending on language. Indeed, they may well be unconscious, pre-verbal, and instantaneous. A characteristic experiment by appraisal theorists, for example, finds that babies at around nine months of age begin to focus their "gaze direction toward novel, unexpected stimuli." This coincides with important cognitive changes in infants that make appraisals of "surprise-inducing" situations more likely.[21]

As this experiment suggests, psychologists working with appraisal theory tend to be more interested in individual and developmental differences than with cultural variations, though they admit that such variation is possible. Appraisal theory postulates that different people may respond to the same *stimuli* differently, depending on their judgments, goals, and values. But if they make the same *appraisal* they will have the same *emotion*. Thus, not everyone will find the same thing surprising, but in general all stimuli that violate "what is expected" will lead to surprise. Neuroscientists working in the cognitive tradition seek the neural substrates involved in such appraisals. David Sander and his associates found, for example, that the brain's amygdala is "a relevance detector"; it helps assess the relevance of a stimulus to an individual's needs and interests.[22]

Affect theory: an anti-cognitivist rebellion

Cognitivism provoked a reaction from researchers who considered it too "rational" a view of emotions. Since emotions were now starting to be defined as kinds of judgments – however immediate and unconscious – some psychologists sought to restore the place of irrationality in theories of human behavior and motivation. They asserted something *before* emotion, even, perhaps, quite separate from emotions. That something was "affect."

A key proponent of affect theory was Silvan Tomkins (d.1991). A psychologist of philosophical bent, he was interested in what lay behind human motivation. One of his students was Paul Ekman, whose "basic emotions" (see above) bear considerable resemblance to Tomkins's list of affects, which are excitement, joy, terror, anger, shame, contempt, distress, surprise.[23] But while Ekman used the word "emotions," Tomkins used the term "affects," which stemmed from the tradition of Wilhelm Wundt and Sigmund Freud. Freud had emphasized drives – above all the sex drive – as the basic motivators of human behavior; Tomkins argued that affects were even stronger motivators. "I view affect as the primary innate biological motivating mechanism, more urgent than drive deprivation and pleasure, and more urgent even than physical pain." This is the opening salvo of an article that Tomkins wrote to sum up his theory in 1984. He explained that breathing is a drive: we need to breathe, and breathing is an essential biological mechanism. But it is not a *motivating* mechanism. What motivates people to breathe, says Tomkins, is the terror that is engendered when their breath is suddenly cut off. A person in, say, a chokehold, is in a state of panic. But when people are gradually deprived of oxygen, as may happen when they are at high altitudes in an airplane without a pressurized cabin or oxygen masks, euphoria sets in and they die with a smile on their lips. Moreover, Tomkins asserts, the terror we feel in a chokehold is the same fear (albeit possibly less intense) that we have when we lose our job or when we hear that we have cancer. The same is true for the other basic motivators: they are activated by a great variety of situations, and they (like terror) are "more urgent" than drives toward pleasure or away from pain. Hunger is satisfied only by food, but excitement has all sorts of objects: food, sex, pleasure, even pain. Without the "affect system," nothing would matter; with it, anything may matter.[24]

Affect is activated by both innate and learned stimuli, but it is innate at the most basic level, when a person is born. Tomkins pointedly meant his theory to challenge the one based on appraisal; his alone, he thought, accounted for both innate and learned responses: "Certainly the infant who emits his birth cry upon exit from the birth canal has not 'appraised' the new environment as a vale of tears before he cries. Equally certain, he will later learn to cry at communications telling of death of a beloved person and this does depend on meaning and its appraisal."[25]

Tomkins hypothesized a neural substrate for affect and for the various levels of stimulation needed to produce the different affects. Affect's intensity depended on what Tomkins called "the density of neural firing." That chokehold suddenly increased the neural firings, activating terror. Abrupt release from the hold made the number of firings swiftly decrease: the result was joy. If the stimulus was more sustained, rather than sudden, the result was the negative affect of distress or, at a higher level of firing, anger.

Although Tomkins's theory borrowed much from James and Darwin, it was more attuned to the social and communicative role of his subject. Treating the cry of the infant, Tomkins observed that it "not only has information of the self and others about a variety of matters needing alleviation, but it also motivates the self and others to reduce it." Discussing the smile, Tomkins hypothesized that the quick reduction in neural firings produced the smile of joy. That experience was then stored in memory and retrieved at the sight of someone else's smiling face. At that point, "the smile of another person is capable of evoking the empathic response." This fits with Tomkins's view that, while words were important (as in Freud's "talking cures" or his method of "free association"), the face and the human ability to perceive its expressions even at a distance played a "critical role ... in human communion."[26]

Affect theory remains important today in some scientific discussions. Jaak Panksepp's work with animals leads him to argue that affect is connected to "deep subcortical brain structures, interacting with primitive viscerosomatic body (core self) representations," whereas cognition "involves the neo-cortical processing of information." He sees affects as "raw" forces that are "resolved" into "higher emotions." Along the same lines, a team led by Nancy Stein argues that affective responses, unlike emotions, are "automatic." They are unconscious reactions to stimuli of high-level "speed, intensity, and duration." In this view, affects are "evolutionary primitive signals that communicate a state of change in physiological reactivity." They differ from emotions because they involve "little or no cognitive evaluation."[27]

The importance of affect theory has been underlined by the publication of a *Companion to Emotion and the Affective Sciences*: among the many brief entries are "affect (philosophical perspectives)," "affect (psychological perspectives)," "affect-as-information model," and "affect bursts." However, this very publication makes clear the controversial nature of the topic. As Louis C. Charland notes, "scientific disputes about the meaning of 'affect' may have escalated to the point where a radical rethinking of the aims and boundaries of 'affective science' is required."[28]

Created emotions: the social constructionist view

While affect theory is a radical statement of emotions' inborn nature, "social constructionism" emphasizes culture and variation. Sociologists, anthropologists, and philosophers were the major formulators of social constructionism as a movement.[29] But the theory of the social construction of emotions was largely the creation of psychologists: they knew and were indebted to appraisal theory, but they also valued "sensitivity to language and awareness of human cultural diversity." In their view, as psychologist James Averill wrote: "Emotions may be conceived of as belief systems or schemas that guide the appraisal of situations, the organization of responses and the self-monitoring (interpretation) of behaviour." Rather than assume that such schemas were universal – "hardwired" into the human psyche in the course of evolution – Averill postulated that they represented learned and internalized social norms. Social constructionists think it very possible that, for example, "happiness" was not an emotion everywhere and at all times. In some places, it might not even be recognized as a concept or word.[30]

If emotions are learned, as social constructionists think, then they are like the lines and actions that an actor memorizes. In the hands of some social constructionists, emotional expression becomes a kind of "practice" or performance.[31] When people express an emotion, they play a role. The role may include gestures, shouts, tears, blushes, widened eyes. It often means saying certain words in particular ways. The role does not feel false – or, at least, not necessarily so. And, given the possibility of "feedback," the performance of an emotion might even induce the feeling of the emotion it intends to demonstrate. Nevertheless, when researchers talk about the "performance of emotion," their emphasis is on the conventional and habitual ways in which people employ emotional language and gestures. Often these involve utilizing "display rules." Here the social constructionist view collaborates with the Darwinian.

Sometimes, the "performance" of emotion is tied to what philosopher J. L. Austin called "performatives."[32] Austin noted that some utterances describe things: "The dog has fur." "The singer is wearing a red dress." These statements are "constatives." But other statements produce transformations. When a judge declares, "The defendant is guilty," he or she has changed the very status of the defendant. The pronouncement of guilt is a "performative."

Hard on the heels of Austin was philosopher Robert Solomon's formulation of emotions: "We might say that the emotions are preverbal analogues of what J. L. Austin called 'performatives' – judgments that *do* something rather than simply describe or evaluate a state of affairs." "That dog scares me" does not describe the dog. We may well be wrong to be scared. But the statement itself is an evaluative judgment that turns the dog into an object of our fear. This idea owes much to the cognitivist tradition, with its emphasis on subjective appraisal. Solomon's view is social constructionist, but with a twist. Rather than speak of the internalization of social norms, Solomon speaks of multiple, often conflicting norms: "We do not create but are taught the forms of interpretation and standards of evaluation which we employ in our emotional judgments ... Our problem, in this society at least, is that there are virtually always alternative sets of such forms and standards."[33]

The performance of emotions, which is largely about how people behave and the impact they have on others, shades quite naturally into concern about the orchestrators of such behaviors. Emotions, in this light, are "managed" from the outside. Just as the members of an orchestra must work hard to play as the conductor directs, so too people must strive to perform their emotions as expected. There are many potential managers: states, employers, families, religious leaders. Researchers do not usually talk about all of these at once, even though Solomon thought they should. In particular, social psychologists have tended to focus on employers, finding, for example, that in general the service industry requires its workers to be cheerful. The classic study of emotional management is by Arlie Hochschild. Most memorably, she observed the training of flight attendants, showing how they were taught not only to smile and look pleasant, but to *feel* smiling and pleasant – to internalize the "emotion rules" that their employer wished them to have. Hochschild called this process "emotional labor" (see Plate 2). Because of their emphasis on social norms, performances, and emotional managers and management, social constructionists seem at first glance to locate emotions *outside* of the body. But this is not so. Emotions are, for them, in the body and mind together. Both absorb social norms, which are thus said to be "embodied."[34]

A few neuroscientists work within the social constructionist paradigm. Making the assumption that the activities of both mind (such as cognition, emotion, and conceptualization) and body (muscle movements, heartbeats, blushes, and so on) must ultimately be traced back to the brain, some neuropsychologists have elaborated a theory they call "the psychological construction of emotions." Psychological constructionism discards distinctions between mind and body: the mind is the "brain and body in context." Furthermore, this theory considers both emotions and cognitions to be the same sort of thing: "conceptualizations." The brain is a "situated conceptualization generator."[35]

Let us unpack this important statement, taking the last word first. If the brain *as a whole* is a "generator" of conceptions, then scientists are wrong to look at this or that structure of the brain as the "site" of this or that emotion. Anatomic brain "regions" are, in the view of psychological constructionists, phantoms.[36] Rather, interactions among neuronal networks across the whole brain are involved in all of its activities. Nor are these activities nicely partitioned among emotion, cognition, memory and perception. All of these things are always involved in the brain's three basic "mental processes," which involve "(1) representing basic sensory information from the world; (2) representing basic interoceptive sensations from the body; and (3) making meaning of internal and external sensations by activating stored representations of prior experience."[37]

That phrase about "making meaning" begins to get at the "conceptualization" part of the notion of a "situated conceptualization generator." We are born with adaptive brain mechanisms that monitor our internal and external environments. The brain retains those perceptions, building up patterns in our memory so that slowly we begin to make sense of the world. We don't initially know that we are hungry, but when we receive milk, we feel satisfied, and gradually "stored representations of prior experience" allow us to put together our need for food with the "conceptualization" we call hunger. Similarly, we do not start life knowing when we are angry, but gradually we come to associate certain sensations that come from our guts and other bodily organs – our interoceptive sensations – with what people around us call anger. Eventually we identify a certain set of sensations as "anger."

But what if people around us – and therefore we – did not identify those sensations, movements, and cries as "anger" but rather as nothing at all? Or what if they were associated with other sensations? This is part of what is meant by saying that the brain is "situated " (Another part is the brain's situatedness in the physiological, interoceptive self.) The brain exists in a social world that gives it language and categories (like "emotion"). That world also suggests goals and values. Emotions are conceptualizations, just as "insect" is a conceptualization. But emotions are unlike insects in that they "reflect the structure of recurring situations that people find important and meaningful within their own cultural context." The emphasis of psychological constructionism is, however, not so much on the cultural context as it is on the brain systems that are involved in "each individual instance of an emotion." Anger is not an "entity," then. It is simply a convenient word for the brain states involved in instances that we have come to associate with one another. Categorization is useful because it prepares us "for situated action." It is good that we know about anger, for example, if we live in a world that uses and finds meaning in that term. And because we are prepared to act on anger (or any other emotion our culture defines), that category affects how we will feel.[38]

Some new work in the genetic sciences partly supports the social constructionist view, adding "environmental constructionism" to the mix. Epigenetics, much like "emotions," has no one definition, but for all scientists it means that genes and genetic mutations do not directly explain all traits. Genes must express themselves – they must produce proteins – to create a trait. But gene expression is often modified or silenced by non-genetic – i.e. epigenetic – factors. Sometimes these changes are heritable.

Epigenetic factors are "environmental" – though the environment may be the cell itself. Most genetic studies focus on the biochemistry of epigenetics. They seek to discover, for example, the effect of methylation on the way a gene functions. Methyl groups (found in various foods) are not part of the DNA, but they may join with a DNA strand (often with a particular carbon atom of cytosine, one of the four nucleotides that make up DNA) with effects both good and ill. This is because they can turn off gene expression or alter it. Nor are methyl groups alone in this. Proteins known as histones are also not part of the genome, and yet they too can regulate genes in certain instances.[39]

This seems far from the topic of emotions. But some scientists touch on the topic when they look for the causes of the biochemical environment in which genes do their work. Observing maternal behavior in rats, one group of researchers has found that the offspring of mothers who excelled in licking and grooming their pups while nursing had different DNA methylation from the pups whose mothers did less licking and grooming. As adults, the rats who had the "more attentive" mothers were less fearful and exhibited less stress than the others. When baby rats with less attentive mothers were reared by more attentive dams, the result was the same as with the biological offspring (and vice versa). Thus, "variations in maternal behavior serve as a mechanism for the nongenomic [or epigenetic] transmission of individual differences in stress reactivity across generations."[40]

The authors of these studies do not speak of "mother love," and indeed those studying rats do not call mother rats "attentive" or "inattentive." But it is hard not to think of human analogues. Siddhartha Mukherjee memorably explains how the starvation of the Dutch in the winter of 1945 affected not only the following generation but the one after that: it altered "the expression of genes involved in metabolism and storage." Everything – "injuries, infections, infatuations; the haunting trill of that particular nocturne" – says Mukherjee, may potentially have an epigenetic effect, even though such effects are utterly unpredictable.[41]

Daniel Smail, too, stresses the potential effect of the environment on the gene, making it more or less likely to assume a particular form of expression. Smail takes a "coevolutionary approach" to the human brain. The brain is plastic, not fixed, and much of its development depends on "genetically informed potentials that must be triggered by environmental influence." Like the psychological constructionists, Smail argues that the brain's neural structures

interact, on a daily basis, with the things we see and hear and feel. They are influenced by neurotransmitters released by the brain-body system and by chemicals that we ingest. What results from the subtle play of chemical and electrical signals that take place in our brain-body are a variety of body states that we feel as drives, appetites, motivations, predispositions, emotions, moods, and phobias.[42]

Smail is not a psychologist; he is a historian glad to bring the theories of science to bear on his profession. Other historians are warier. Yet all, as partakers of modern culture and its scientific bent, draw to one degree or another on the assumptions, vocabulary, and interests of science even as they seek to craft new approaches and insights appropriate to the larger story of mankind. Let us, then, turn to some key historical approaches to emotions.

2
Approaches

Theories, whether scientific, philosophical, or theological, do not remain the preserve of specialists alone. They diffuse into other fields and other audiences, and they help shape how people think. This is certainly the case for historians of emotions. In this chapter, we survey the chief foundational approaches to the topic. Most were articulated by a particular historian but soon became part of a larger historical discussion. In this relatively new field, however, even the "foundations" are quite recent. At the end of the chapter, we compare the approaches by applying them to the same concrete instance: the Declaration of Independence of the United States.

Beginnings

Historians have always talked about emotions, which help spice up narratives and explain motivations. Thus, when the ancient Greek historian Herodotus (5th c. BCE) talked about

Darius's expedition into Scythia, he did not need to put the Persian ruler on the couch to say that he was anxious to have his revenge." Whether or not vengeance inspired Darius, it made sense to Herodotus' readers, for whom the desire for revenge was a well-understood motive for war.

With the advent of cultural history in the nineteenth century, some historians found ways to characterize the emotional temperament of entire societies. A particularly influential practitioner was Johan Huizinga, whose *Waning of the Middle Ages* was published in Dutch in 1919. For Huizinga, the Middle Ages represented the "childhood" of man, and the late Middle Ages was its final, luxuriant expression:

> To the world when it was half a thousand years younger, the outlines of all things seemed more clearly marked than to us ... All experience had yet to the minds of men the directness and absoluteness of the pleasure and pain of child-life ... All things in life were of a proud or cruel publicity ... All things presenting themselves to the mind in violent contrasts and impressive forms, lent a tone of excitement and of passion to everyday life and tended to produce that perpetual oscillation between despair and distracted joy, between cruelty and pious tenderness which characterize life in the Middle Ages.

In Huizinga's day, the "childlike mind" – the "primitive mind" – was a widely-shared construct; anthropologists, too, talked about it. The Middle Ages was the Western historians' equivalent of tribal cultures.[1]

French historian Lucien Febvre read Huizinga's book during the rise of Nazism. Co-founder with Marc Bloch of the so-called *Annales* school, Febvre was interested in the underlying, enduring structures of the past. He and his colleagues belittled political history: it was *histoire événementielle*, the story of mere "events." One important structure was *mentalité*: the slow-moving human mind as it revealed itself in emotions and attitudes. Febvre, reflecting on both Huizinga's words and the theories of emotions of some of his psychologist colleagues, thought that emotions always rumbled under the surface of civilized life. Sometimes, however, they emerged with ferocity: during the Middle Ages, for example; and again in Febvre's own day, when German armies had taken Poland and Czechoslovakia and were occupying France. Febvre thought that emotions would erupt again and again unless historians understood their vagaries. He called for a new kind of history: "The history of hate, the history of fear, the history of cruelty, the history of love."[2]

Unknown to Febvre, a German sociologist, Norbert Elias, had in effect already answered his call in 1939. While Elias had much the same vision of the Middle Ages as Huizinga and Febvre, going so far as to claim that its "people are wild, cruel, prone to violent outbreaks and abandoned to the joy of the moment," Elias did not think that the Nazis heralded a new age of untrammeled emotion. Rather, he considered the Germans to be an exception to the general course of Western civilization. The larger pattern saw a transformation from impulse to restraint, from lack of civility to good manners, from the sway of primitive drives to the tyranny of the super-ego. The agent of change was the absolutist state of the sixteenth and seventeenth centuries typified by the court of Louis XIV, whose monopoly on force made capricious violence moot. (Germany had not had an absolutist regime, and therefore its evolution was stunted.) Influenced by Sigmund Freud and Max Weber, Elias considered modern people to be conscience-ridden cogs in a complex bureaucracy. At the same time, their conscience rendered them capable of restrained emotions and finer feelings.[3]

Insofar as anyone worked on the history of emotions before the 1980s or so, he or she tended to find their guides in Huizinga, Elias, and Febvre. After 1980, their approaches and methods built on the cognitive revolution and the social constructionist points of view. Two scholarly streams – histories of theories of emotion and psychohistory – remained largely independent of this story, however. The first was, and largely remains, a separate field, part of intellectual history. A good example is the ambitious study published in 1937 by H. Norman Gardiner and his colleagues: it begins with the theories of Heraclitus (c.500 BCE) and ends with those of the 1930s. New scholarship in this vein continues to be written, some of which – such as the recent book on medieval emotion theories by Carla Casagrande and Silvana Vecchio – also place theories within their larger historical contexts. A few very recent books integrate theories of emotions with "lived" emotions.[4] The second independent stream, psychohistory, draws on the insights of psychoanalysis. Quite popular in the 1970s, this approach retains some adherents today. Ludwig Janus, for example, asserts that "the human baby is born physically but remains emotionally in a fetal realm of experience." He postulates that "tribal cultures" never allow for development beyond these fetal stances, while Western culture has found ways to "facilitate operational thinking as well as a sense of separation between I and you." Some historians – Lyndal Roper is one – draw on psychoanalysis without being "psychohistorians." Roper uses Freudian insights as one tool among many others, including anthropology and literary criticism, to bring early modern subjectivities closer to modern sensibilities.[5]

Emotionology

Even before Febvre, and certainly thereafter, various historians wrote about emotions in history.[6] Yet, it is fair to say that the "modern field" as it is known today was launched in 1985 in an article written by historian Peter Stearns and his then-wife historian-psychiatrist Carol Zisowitz Stearns. The Stearnses proposed that historians look not at "real emotions," which, in their view, were largely universal and unchanging, but at standards of emotions – "emotionology," as they put it – which changed over time. In an article announcing their ideas, they used two epigrams. The second was the composite definition of "real emotion" offered by the Kleinginnas (discussed in Chapter 1). The first was a definition of their neologism:

> Emotionology: the attitudes or standards that a society, or a definable group within a society, maintains toward basic emotions and their appropriate expression; ways that institutions reflect and encourage these attitudes in human conduct, e.g. courtship practices as expressing the valuation of affect in marriage, or personnel workshops as reflecting the valuation of anger in job relationships.[7]

As this definition shows, the Stearnses accepted the notion of basic emotions. As set forth by psychologist Paul Ekman and others in the 1970s, these were universal and unchanging. But the Stearnses found a way to reconcile that universalist view with a social constructionist position. Rather than see a contradiction between biology and society, the Stearnses carefully separated out what in their view was biological – basic emotions – from what was social. If basic emotions never changed, standards for how and where people should reveal and express them changed fast. Emotions, as Arlie Hochschild had shown, were "managed." The Stearnses proposed emotionology as a way to discover the management protocols of the past.

Their method was straightforward: they drew systematically on the advice literature that began to be written for Western middle-class audiences in the eighteenth century and has continued apace to the present. In a book on anger, the Stearnses made their technique clear. First, they gathered a huge dossier of sources – mainly advice literature aimed at audiences in the North Atlantic United States, but also some popular magazine fiction and so on – from the nineteenth and twentieth centuries. Second, they read what the sources had to say about managing anger in two contexts: at home – among parents, children, and spouses – and in the workplace. As they read, the Stearnses paid close attention to the dates of the manuals in order to discern periods of stasis and moments of change in emotional standards. Third, the Stearnses ascertained from a different set of sources – personal writings such as letters and diaries – whether the emotionology of a given period had impact on "real emotions." From these sources, they sought to explore how real families behaved and how real workers and managers acted, arguing that new standards and behaviors had consequences, in a kind of feedback mechanism, for how people really felt. Here emotional management and genuine feelings met and influenced one another. Thus, emotions were not, in the end, entirely hardwired and changeless for the Stearnses. Emotion rules had a kind of dynamism: they "shaped," they even "launched" felt emotions. Once emotionology had been absorbed and put into practice by eager readers of advice manuals, it became a form of sincere emotional expression. Finally, the Stearnses considered the multiple factors that caused emotionology to change. They argued that social and economic shifts, together with new trends in scientific and other "expert" thought, determined what the advice books would say. In this sense, theories of emotions were inseparable from lived feelings. Darwin's "survival of the fittest," for example, inspired an emotionology that encouraged competitive behavior in the workplace. At the same time, the hypotheses of social Darwinism were themselves influenced by the needs of industrial factories.[8]

The result of the Stearnses' work was a history of clear causes, effects, and turning points. Let us consider briefly the story of anger, at least for the American North Atlantic. Up to the 1860s, Victorian-style advice books condemned anger in every form. But during the period 1860 to 1940, manuals recognized that it was unrealistic to restrain anger entirely. Without quite praising anger, the new emotionology allowed for it, especially by advocating its appropriate channeling in boys, who were to be aggressive and energetic in venues outside the home. The same "realism enter[ed], more hesitantly, into marital advice as well." But here the "realism" centered on sex rather than anger, counseling that "quarrels or anger must be understood as the symptoms of a bad sexual adjustment." During this same period, some popular literature began to propose strategies to reduce anger in marriages, and this became a dominant theme in post-1940s emotionology. In the end, the new standards for anger, combined with consumerism and other shifts in culture and ideology, caused a slow "effect on personality style." Parents "stepped up their attempts to control their own anger." Women "reaped some benefit from the new, albeit guarded, sanction to express anger at home." Even public policy responded to the new expectations, as in the development of no-fault divorce, which bypassed anger in favor of amicable settlement.[9]

Leaving anger behind, Peter Stearns and his student Timothy Haggerty used the same techniques to study the emotionology of fear. They found that in the period 1850 to 1900, advice manuals assumed that children were naturally fearless unless inculcated with fears by ignorant adults. At the same time, "moralistic children's stories urged an active confrontation with fear as part of a successful boyhood." The key word for men and boys was "courage." (In the same set of sources, girls, sustained by their religious beliefs, went to their early deaths without fear, while women waited patiently for their courageous men to come home from war.) To inculcate these virtues in both sons and daughters, mothers were warned against using fear to discipline their children. The "boogeyman" was banished, and fear in general was distrusted because it hindered reasonable action. Nevertheless, around 1950 this emotionology changed: children were seen as born full of fears. Advice manuals told parents to reassure and protect their children from fearful situations.[10]

These early, pioneering works in the history of emotions inspired – and continue to inspire – numerous scholars. While Carol Stearns stopped writing histories, Peter Stearns continues to study emotions. Although he began by thinking of emotionology as a largely private matter, with only indirect impact on public policy (as with the implementation of no-fault divorce), he gradually came to concentrate on political institutions. Thus, he relied on his findings with Haggerty in a later book on fear and public policy. Stearns noted that in the wake of the 1941 Japanese bombing of Pearl Harbor, Americans denied feeling fear, as would be expected from the advice books that they were brought up with. That is why Franklin Delano Roosevelt's first presidential inaugural address in 1933 could belittle fear: "The only thing we have to fear is fear itself."

But after 1950, as fears became taboo, they simultaneously grew more threatening. Even though the post-war period in the United States should have been reassuring – with its seat belts, medicines, and bicycle helmets – Americans never felt more menaced and fearful. Thus, when planes manned by terrorists hit New York City in 2001, Americans did not react as they had to the attack on Pearl Harbor. To the contrary: "Quite obviously, fear hit New York City," writes Stearns. And not just New York. New solutions were designed to be reassuring, but ended up ironically fanning the flames of fear: a new department of homeland security was established, the war on terrorism was launched, and "ominous" color-coded warnings stoked existing worries. For Stearns, the study of emotionology was crucial for understanding political policies at the highest level. The emotionology of fear that developed "initially in personal and familial settings some decades back ... began to shape public responses to threat."[11]

Today, emotionology has taken on meanings apart from advice books and in fields both historical and non-historical. As an example of the non-historical, consider social anthropologist

Inger-Lise Lien, who speaks of "gang emotionology" to describe violent men and boys who are driven by anxiety but never allow themselves to express it: "This is the morality, or what we have called the emotionology of criminality, or gang emotionology. This emotionology is about feelings that someone *ought to have had* in particular situations, and not about the feelings someone really has."[12]

Historians have adopted Stearns's methods for a variety of purposes. Susan Matt's study of homesickness shows a sea change in attitudes toward that emotion. In eighteenth- and nineteenth-century America, longing for home and homeland was valued and freely expressed. In the twentieth century, it came to be considered a sign of weakness and, indeed, lost its status as an emotion. Drawing on advice manuals and other sources, Matt argued that "the history of homesickness recovers the story of how Americans learned to manage their feelings, but beyond that, it reveals how Americans learned habits of individualism that supported capitalist activity." Thus, even in the case of homesickness, emotions changed in accordance with social and economic needs. A similar point was made by Ute Frevert and her team in Berlin, who studied the ways in which children's literature taught feelings. Shifts corresponded to changing values within advice manuals which, in turn, mirrored the values of society at large. Stearns himself is no longer tied to advice manuals, more recently looking at statistics to discuss "the gulf between measureable advances [in the quality of life] and perceived happiness." Here he harks back to a theme that bedeviled Freud and Elias: modernity itself brings discontent. For Stearns, however, the problem is an emotionology that constrains people "to seem (and, if possible, to actually be) cheerful and happy."[13]

Summing up recent work in the history of emotions, Susan Matt speaks of a chronological progression: "First came those who looked at emotional ideals; later came historians who tried to reconstruct emotional experiences and the differences between conventions and individual feelings. They were joined by those who suggested that there were many competing sets of expectations and rules within a single society ... Gradually a consensus emerged that although one could not study emotional life without understanding the social rules governing it, neither should one explore those rules without at least trying to assess individual reactions to them." Emotionology was the first stage; the second was that of William Reddy; and the third that of Barbara Rosenwein. Let us continue our survey by following Matt's sequence and turn next to William Reddy.[14]

Emotional regimes and emotives

A professor of anthropology as well as history, William M. Reddy was the scholar Matt alluded to when she spoke of "historians who tried to reconstruct emotional experiences and the differences between conventions and individual feelings." Reddy first announced his approach in an article, "Against Constructionism," in a 1997 issue of *Current Anthropology*, thus engaging an audience more interested in human nature than in human history.

Reddy was against constructionism because he found it radically relativist. He argued that if our values, thoughts, genders, and emotions are all socially constructed, then there is no way to critique any society. His point was that anything we say will itself be socially constructed and thus of no greater value than the social constructions – political systems, attitudes toward and treatment of women, and so on – that we critique. Moreover, noted Reddy, if everything is socially constructed, there is no way to account for change. This had not been an issue for Stearns: for him, social, economic, and intellectual transformations opened the way to modifications in emotionology. Reddy had a different theory of change, one that made emotions themselves its agents. "A coherent account of emotional change must find a dynamic, a vector of alteration. But this dynamic can be found in the very character of emotional expression." Whether uttered or acted out, emotional expressions have the "unique capacity to alter what they 'refer' to or what they 'represent' – a capacity which makes them neither 'constative' nor 'performative' utterances but a third type of communicative utterance." This third type Reddy called "emotives."[15]

What did Reddy mean? His term was a riff on Austin's notion of "performatives," utterances with transformative effect (see Chapter 1). Reddy asserted that emotions were similarly transmuting, and he coined the neologism "emotives" to express this idea. Emotives worked in two ways: they changed those to whom they were addressed, and they altered the person speaking them. Furthermore, Reddy argued that it was possible to judge societies by how fully they permitted emotives. Societies that allowed for "emotional freedom," welcoming emotives and tolerating their ambiguity and volatility, were better than those that induced "emotional suffering" by limiting emotives.

Reddy defined "emotions" as "goal-relevant activations of thought material that exceed the translating capacity of attention within a short time horizon." Some features of this definition are familiar. Cognitivists talk about aims and goals, and Reddy's reference to "thought material" puts his definition in the cognitivist camp as well as that of the psychological constructionists, for whom emotions are among the "conceptualizations" that the brain generates. But when Reddy said that these cognitions "exceed the translating capacity of attention within a short time horizon," he was drawing on an aspect of affect theory that led him to his hypothesis of "emotives." Consider the utterance "I love you." For Reddy, this statement is the result of the activation of thought material that we have "translated" into an emotional speech act. In fact, when we make that utterance, we have a whole array of feelings that saying "I love you" barely expresses. Unable to attend to all of them (since they "exceed the translating capacity of attention"), we focus on "love," at least during the "short time horizon" in which we are putting it into an utterance. But as we do so, we activate other goal-relevant feelings.[16]

Emotives – emotions enacted in speech – are, therefore, different from other utterances. They describe an emotional state (it's a "fact" that we love someone), they alter their object (who is not moved by being told she is loved?), and they call up a whole panoply of feelings in the person making the utterance. As Reddy puts it: the emotive "has an exploratory and a self-altering effect on the activated thought material of emotion." "I love you" activates new thoughts: perhaps, "I love you more than I ever thought possible;" or "Well, do I really love you?" For Reddy, every emotive is both sincere and insincere. It is sincere because it accords with one goal. But since people have more than one goal, the same emotive is insincere in connection with a conflicting goal. "I love you," yes; but I also want to be by myself – or with someone else.

Love is one emotion, but it is also protean. The same is true of any emotion: they *all* "exceed the translation capacity of attention." When expressed, *all of them* are emotives. Left to their own devices, emotives would lead to constant self-exploration. But they are not left alone; they are subject to "emotional regimes," namely, "the set of normative emotions and the official rituals, practices, and emotives that express and inculcate them." Reddy elaborated on this: "Emotional control is the real site of the exercise of power: politics is just a process of determining who must repress as illegitimate, who must foreground as valuable, the feelings and desires that come up for them in given contexts and relationships." Because the emotional regime, almost by definition, does not allow emotives their full potential, it creates the conditions for an *emotional refuge*: "a relationship, ritual, or organization ... that provides safe release from prevailing emotional norms and allows relaxation of emotional effort ... which may shore up or threaten the existing emotional regime." If the emotional regime is too controlling, if it impedes the self-altering effects of emotives and prevents people from changing their goals, then it not only causes emotional suffering, but also creates an emotional refuge possibly poised to do it harm.[17]

In *The Navigation of Feeling*, Reddy argued that the French Revolution was an emotional revolution. The emotionally repressive court of the French king induced acute emotional suffering. In a kind of dialectic, people sought an emotional refuge where passionate feelings of every kind would be highly valued and explored. The refuge took many forms – salons, theaters, and clubs – but all fostered what historians call "sentimentalism." Here social hierarchies broke down in favor of "companionate equality ... A new optimism about human nature spread widely, an optimism based in part on new confidence in the power of human reason, in part on the belief that certain natural sentiments, sentiments that everyone was capable of feeling, were the foundation of virtue and could serve as the basis for political reform,"[18]

In effect, the French Revolution was the triumph of that emotional refuge: it overthrew the repressive emotional regime of the court and installed sentimentalism in its place. But this new emotional regime induced its own forms of emotional suffering. It demanded such high-flown, passionate emotions, that no one could possibly sustain them for long. Soon, it created (in reaction) the Directory, which ended the reign of sentimentalism. Napoleon's rule was more in accord with the nature of emotives, offering them various outlets and providing multiple goals. The succeeding period – Romanticism – also allowed for emotives, exploring them in literature, art, and private life. But in other spheres – the "male" spheres of morality and public policy – emotions were devalued as weak and inferior to reason. True: reason, too, was weak, likely to be overwhelmed by passion. But that was acceptable as long as men "concealed their lapses effectively." This was the new, post-sentimental "normative emotional management regime," and it proved to be exceptionally stable, persisting into our own era.[19]

In a subsequent book, *The Making of Romantic Love*, Reddy dropped the carefully defined terms of his earlier work. Nevertheless, his schema remained, particularly in his discussion of the Western experience. Here the dynamic may be analyzed (although Reddy does not use the old vocabulary) more or less in the following manner: until the early twelfth century, medieval aristocrats in the south of France were largely free to change their goals and to explore their emotions. In the world of love, sex, and marriage, this system allowed for great flexibility, many changes of objects, many fluctuating goals. The "longing for association," which Reddy here postulates as a universal emotion, was fulfilled in numerous ways under these circumstances. All this was challenged by the Catholic Church, newly reformed in the eleventh century. The Church demanded written claims and permanent marriages. It condemned sexual desire, calling it a polluting appetite. It created, in effect, a new and powerful emotional regime. And, as we might expect, it engendered an emotional refuge: the invention of "romantic love" in poetry. In this refuge, sex was lauded as good when combined with love so self-sacrificing and so spiritual as to make it holy. That refuge, however, turned out to be as limiting as the regime, setting up impossible expectations for unwavering love within monogamous relationships. We continue to live with its unhappy legacy. But other cultures never had it. Reddy's book compares the European experience with concurrent South Asian and Japanese cultures, which never separated sexual desire from spiritual practices, and thus always had multiple ways to express their longing for association.[20]

Reddy's work has influenced scholars in many different fields. Cultural anthropologist Ferdiansyah Thajib speaks of the Indonesian Muslim queen community "navigating" among its conflicting emotions.[21] Sociologist Valérie de Courville Nicol finds emotives helpful in explaining "the production of social conformity." When there is a conflict between conventional goals and the desire to deviate, "conventional emotives" provide a way to resolve the matter by promising "pleasurable social rewards."[22] But, above all, Reddy's work has inspired historians. Nicole Eustace, for example, argues that the American Revolution, like the French, made the "passions and feelings of mankind" the "basis for natural equality and the firmest foundation for natural rights." However, she makes "emotives" less a means of self-exploration than a force for social ratification, contestation, and alteration. On the one hand, she argues, uttered emotions served to notify others of status differences, of the loci of power, and of challenges to them. (Here Eustace draws on Reddy's dictum about the politics of emotion management.) On the other hand, she finds that sentimentalism was not a "refuge" in colonial America but rather, in the version in which it crossed the Atlantic (from England, via the poetry of Alexander Pope), it was the starting point for a series of highly contentious discussions about the role of the passions in virtue, both personal and social. In this way, Eustace shows how emotions "performed" a variety of tasks. When they expressed their love, "eighteenth-century Anglo-Americans engaged simultaneously in the search for personal fulfillment, the effort to assert social status, and the quest to stabilize community." Similarly, "expressions and descriptions of anger provided a key means of negotiating status, of establishing honor and dishonor, in the fluid colonial world."[23]

Emotional communities

Susan Matt was doubtless thinking of Barbara H. Rosenwein when she spoke of historians "who suggested that there were many competing sets of expectations and rules within a single society." In an article published in 2002 devoted to assessing the history of emotions as it stood at that time, Rosenwein proposed that historians study coexisting "emotional communities." As she explained,

> [Emotional communities] are precisely the same as social communities – families, neighborhoods, parliaments, guilds, monasteries, parish church memberships – but the researcher looking at them seeks above all to uncover systems of feeling: what these communities (and the individuals within them) define and assess as valuable or harmful to them; the evaluations that they make about others' emotions; the nature of the affective bonds between people that they recognize; and the modes of emotional expression that they expect, encourage, tolerate, and deplore.[24]

Rosenwein hoped that this new focus would overcome four "roadblocks" then impeding the history of emotions. First, and most important, was Elias's civilizing process. Rosenwein, a medievalist, was unhappy that modernists – who at that time constituted the majority of those dealing with the history of emotions – had wittingly or unwittingly accepted Elias's schema, treating the Middle Ages as a kind of emotionally primitive society on which modernity constructed itself. Ancient historians claimed a "civilizing process" for their own period.[25] And some medievalists wanted to push back the beginning of the civilizing process to as early as the tenth century.[26] Rosenwein thought that the whole idea of such a process was wrong-headed. There was no age of untrammeled emotions, no "childhood of mankind." The only "age of childhood" was biological childhood itself. If adults behaved (in the historian's judgmental view) "like" children, that behavior should be appreciated and assessed as an emotional style with meaningful purposes and traditions, ways of communicating, and modes of expression. One might indeed find groups – in the Middle Ages and thereafter as well – that valued loud, seemingly impulsive, seemingly (to us) coarse and violent emotional displays, but these were in themselves valued modes of expression within a group. The researcher's task was to understand why they were valued and to explore how they worked.

The second barrier was "emotionology" as it was then defined by the Stearnses. If emotionology could be discovered only in advice books for the modern middle classes, then in effect there could be no emotionology – no standards for emotional expression – until the eighteenth century when such manuals began to appear. This was too limiting. Rosenwein thought that there was emotionology long before modernity. Third was Reddy's idea of emotional regimes. Without denying the importance of elites and political power, Rosenwein was more interested in the multiple emotional solutions that people created even within a seemingly hegemonic system. Finally, she was dissatisfied with the performative view, which treated emotions as displays and rituals. As we shall see, that approach is more all-embracing today than it was in 2002. At the time, it was largely limited to the emotions of medieval rulers. In Rosenwein's view, emotions were far more than forms of non-verbal political communication.

In her subsequent work, Rosenwein explored the potential of emotional communities to illuminate the history of emotions. As she did so, she jettisoned part of her original formulation. Rather than consider neighborhoods and parish churches as examples of emotional communities, she came to treat them as shared spaces that helped reveal the characteristics of a given group. People from one community might rub shoulders with those from another; but, on the whole, behaviors, attitudes and feelings were shaped by the community of which people were a part. For example, in the fifteenth century, when one member of the restrained and reserved English Paston family visited the exuberant court of Burgundy, he was much amused. But he did not become *part* of that very different emotional community.[27]

Rosenwein was influenced by cognitivist and social constructionist theories of emotion. However, insofar as they were rooted in a notion of society in the singular, she parted company with them, stressing diversity in every society. To get at the differences and similarities among emotional communities, Rosenwein worked – far more than either Stearns or Reddy – with emotion words and their sequences. She noted that people rarely expressed single emotions but rather strung them together, one after another. They felt, say, angry, then sad, then ashamed, and perhaps, at the end of the series, benevolent. The Stearnses' research largely involved tracking changes in standards for "basic emotions" – fear or anger, for example. Reddy, by contrast, saw emotives as so elastic that he hardly dealt with individual emotions at all, working rather with categories like "emotional" or "non-emotional." Rosenwein sought to uncover systems of feeling from words and word usage. As she put it, "Because emotions are inchoate until they are given names, emotional vocabularies are excep- tionally important for the ways in which people understand, express, and indeed 'feel' their emotions." In this, her work accorded with the theory of psychological constructionism, which argues that the brain's circuitry is shaped in part by ambient emotion words and their associations. It is true that people express their emotions through bodily gestures, blush- ing, tears, facial expressions and so on. But, on the whole, historians know about even these movements from the words in their primary source texts.[28]

Even the word "emotion" should not be taken for granted, as Thomas Dixon has amply demonstrated. Non-western soci- eties have no word that exactly tracks what we – Occidentals – mean by emotions, and even we are not always in agreement about its meaning (as seen in Chapter 1). However, this issue is less problematic within the Western tradition. Already the ancient Greeks had a term (*pathe*) that embraced many of the terms (anger, fear, and so on) that are associated with emotions today. The *pathe* were translated into Latin in the heyday of Rome; and that Latin vocabulary – infused with new meanings and valuations, and modified in many ways – was transmitted to European societies and languages in the Middle Ages and beyond.[29]

In her first book on the subject, *Emotional Communities in the Early Middle Ages*, Rosenwein, rejecting the notion of basic emotions, began with the emotion "word-hoard" avail- able in the ancient world.[30] In the first century BCE, Cicero had explained the Stoic view of emotions and gave numerous examples in his *Tusculan Disputations*. Mining this discus- sion, Rosenwein came up with a list – admittedly incomplete

– of Latin emotion words. She showed how Christian thinkers, working with a new set of values, not only changed the significance of Cicero's terms but also dropped some of them and added others. In her later book, *Generations of Feeling*, she suggested that the emotion words of some communities might be discovered by finding words associated with the heart, mind, and spirit. Of course, that depended on whether a particular community located emotions in such places!

Emotional Communities used a variety of approaches. In the first chapter for example, it looked at sixth- and seventh-century epitaphs carved on the tombs of the dead at three Gallic cities: Trier, Clermont, and Vienne. These epitaphs used standard formulae, but, in Rosenwein's view, that was no drawback, for those very commonplaces revealed the emotions that people expected and valued. Furthermore, as she discovered, the boilerplate in one city was not the same as in others; there were regional differences. A typical epitaph at Trier expressed much family affection: "Here lies in peace the sweetest child, ... Arablia, his daughter, who lived 7 years, ... months and 10 days." But at Clermont, by contrast, no epitaph spoke of "sweet" children.[31]

While tombs revealed only the emotions of mourning, other chapters in the same book sought to describe emotional expectations, valuations, and modes of expression more generally. In a chapter on Pope Gregory the Great (d.604), Rosenwein explored the writings of one man, making the assumption that Gregory's ideas resonated with his audience. This was a very different technique from that of either Stearns or Reddy. It was also different from that of psychohistorians, who would have been interested in Gregory's emotional life per se. Rosenwein was interested in Gregory's emotional community: she argued that his words expressed the views and values of the group he was addressing. Subsequent chapters used a great variety of sources to consider different communities from around Gregory's time or a bit later. The result was a panorama of diverse, yet largely co-existing emotional communities in the sixth and seventh centuries.

That time period was very narrow. *Emotional Communities* demonstrated that medieval people were not childlike or impulsive – even in the early Middle Ages, generally considered the most barbaric age of all. But that did not speak to the grand thesis of Elias, which stretched from the medieval to the early modern period. Nor did the book deal much with the question of change. These were the issues taken up in Rosenwein's *Generations of Feeling* (2016). Here the canvas was vast, going from the seventh to the seventeenth century. But the subjects were limited and precise. For each broadly defined historical period taken up in a chapter, Rosenwein discussed two or more emotional communities. They persisted over time, but they also changed. Some sprouted new shoots, or sub-communities. For example, the Levellers, seventeenth-century English political radicals, formed a sub-community hived off from the Puritans. They re-purposed the emotions they had expressed in their mostly independent dissenting churches. Rather than call only for freedom of religion, as independent Puritan churches invariably did, they campaigned for "that opportunity God hath given us to make this nation free and happy."[32] In Leveller vocabulary, both freedom and happiness had emotional valence. (It is no accident that the pair found their way into the Declaration of Independence, as we shall see below.) Other emotional communities changed because they adapted to new circumstances. A few did not, leading to their marginalization or even disappearance. Rosenwein likened emotional communities within the body politic to "genome mosaicism" in the biological human body. Their sheer variety made possible new responses in new contexts. Even so, they used older elements, seen above all in emotional sequences. For example, not only were the individual emotions revealed by fifteenth-century mystic Margery Kempe similar to those expressed by seventeenth-century Puritans, but they also followed a similar order.

In light of all of this, Rosenwein concluded that there was no grand shift between the pre- and early-modern periods, no "civilizing process." There was only reshuffling, repurposing, and recombining of old elements under new circumstances. And there was rethinking. *Generations of Feeling* interleaved four chapters on emotional communities with five on the major theories of emotion that pertained to the chronological periods under discussion. That move signaled a major shift: Rosenwein did not wish to deny the impact of modern scientific thought on her own approaches, but she now recognized that modern theories were historically contingent, subject to refinement and even rejection in the decades to come. She realized that earlier theories of emotion were similarly imbedded in their own eras, and they inspired – as well as were shaped by – the emotional communities of the past.

Like emotionology and emotives, the idea of "emotional communities" has influenced other scholars. In their edited collection on love in modern Africa, Jennifer Cole and Lynn M. Thomas stressed a variety of communities of feeling, avoided any "grand narrative," and traced history in small "increments of transformation and change." The essays in their book showed how African men – and, above all, women – variously employed Western notions of romantic love in creative self-fashioning, neither rejecting nor adopting it wholesale. In a study of young women's diaries in early American history, Martha Tomhave Blauvelt organized her work by "the emotional communities which women entered and left." Joanne McEwan observed that the size of an emotional community was key. Although the larger community in eighteenth-century Scotland strongly disapproved of infanticide, nevertheless "as we narrow in on smaller spaces and individual exchanges within communities, we can see individuals exerting agency and making decisions about their emotional responses." Thus, "the loyalties and affective attachments of family members to each other often trumped adherence to the acceptable 'feeling rules,' or emotional scripts, prescribed by wider community standards." McEwan assimilated this point to Reddy's notion of an "emotional refuge." Another historian, Barbara Newman, used "emotional communities" in two ways: as a near-equivalent of "textual communities" and as a term to describe people who share emotional values and norms. For the first, she noted how the textual tradition of the ancient Roman author Ovid – as it was elaborated and studied in the Middle Ages – shaped the emotional community of the male lover in an anonymous medieval love-letter collection, while the textual traditions of Christianity informed that of the female voice. For the second point, she suggested that "although they began from different starting points, the lovers converged to form a private emotional community of

two, with their own pet names and intimate quirks." Steven
Mullaney saw the Elizabethan theater as a "kind of affective
laboratory, an instantilation of drama oriented toward the
location, exploration, and exploitation of those faultlines
and dissonances of feeling that characterized the emotional
communities of post-Reformation England."[33]

Emotions as performances

The suggestion that theater is an "affective laboratory" develops
an idea first popularized in the 1950s: that people "put on a
show" when they interact with others. In 1955, J.L. Austin
coined the word performative; soon thereafter, sociologist
Erving Goffman published a study of how we present ourselves
to others with a chapter on "performances." Anthropologists
such as Clifford Geertz picked up on the idea, as did feminist
theorists like Judith Butler, who argued that people performed
their gender. Historians were quick to add their voices to the
mix. As we have seen, Reddy, too, modeled his "emotives"
on the term "performatives."[34]

Gerd Althoff was one of the first historians to approach
emotional display as a dramatic, ritualized performance. For
him the impetus came largely from two avenues: first, the
ongoing debate among German historians about the origins
and significance of the modern state; second, the work of
literary scholars on the many emotions – tears, love, joy – in
medieval poetry. The two avenues merged at medieval courts:
those centered on kings were sites of state formation; those
organized by aristocrats were hubs of literary activity. When
Althoff began to write, many historians were declaring that
there had been no state during the Middle Ages. There had
been no bureaucracy, no theory of sovereignty, no citizens.
There was no entity that monopolized power. There were only
personal ties and practices: fealty, protection, honor, favor, and
disfavor. All of those depended on a ruler's charisma and a cult
of personality. They depended, too, on public expressions of
emotion. It was in this context that Huizinga called attention
to the "exaggerated" tears and raptures of the late Middle
Ages and judged them "childish." His verdict accorded with
the general idea that insofar as there was a medieval "state,"

it was itself a sort of embryo.[35] Yet, as Althoff observed, when literary scholars found emotions in courtly poetry, they explored them as serious topics. He proposed to follow their lead regarding the emotions expressed by rulers and, by doing so, to reassess medieval governance.[36]

Althoff argued that seemingly arbitrary and impulsive bursts of emotion in fact followed well-understood, if unwritten, "rules of the game." His method offered a new "approach to the constitutional history of the Middle Ages." Noting that medieval communication generally took place not through written texts or spoken words but rather via demonstrative acts – kneeling in fealty, bowing in prayer, rituals of greeting and leave-taking – Althoff proposed to reinterpret emotional "outbursts" as political announcements (see Plate 3). They followed well-honed patterns with clear meanings in their own context. In effect, public emotional displays were rituals that signaled messages to their audience. Such "signals prevented misunderstandings and surprises, offering to public interactions the measure of security urgently needed by a stateless arms-bearing society." In the place of a medieval "state," Althoff argued for a different sort of political system of considerable sophistication.

By way of example, Althoff considered an emotional confrontation between Bishop Bernward of Hildesheim and the nuns of Gandersheim that took place in the year 1000. When the bishop insisted, against the wishes of the archbishop, to consecrate Gandersheim's new church, the nuns, who were on the side of the archbishop, protested. At Mass, according to Bernward's biographer, "they threw down their offerings angrily and with incredible fury, and uttered savage curses against the bishop." The bishop, for his part, "was deeply shocked and, overcome by tears according to the example of the Good Shepherd [namely Christ], who prayed for his tormenters, deplored the malevolent fury of the women," and continued with the Mass. But, as Althoff pointed out, hurling down objects, cursing, and weeping were not impulsive behaviors. Rather, they were well-recognized signs of dissent. The nuns were protesting the bishop's rights over their convent. The bishop's behavior, in turn, was "part of a staging calculated for effect. His 'imitation of Christ' was demonstrative proof that he was truly the Pastor."

The same sorts of argument should be made. Althoff thought, for reports of public joy or tears. When Emperor Otto III wanted to make peace with rebels at Rome, he spoke conciliatory words to them. "Are you not my Romans? For your sake I left my homeland and my kinsmen; for love of you I rejected my Saxons and all the Germans, my own blood, altogether." His listeners were "moved to tears and promised satisfaction." These tears were not impulsive outbursts; they were signals of reconciliation.[37] Althoff argued that even if the sources exaggerated, indeed, even if they "made things up," one fact remained: writers did not tell their tales in a void. Their narratives had to have verisimilitude even when they did not report the "absolute truth." That meant that historians could use such accounts to discover some of the emotional standards of the time. In effect, they provided templates for emotionology, even if they were not advice books.

In fact, however, there were advice books in the Middle Ages, among them the so-called *Mirrors of Princes*. These treatises told rulers to show clemency and mildness. Althoff was interested in how such virtues were staged, finding that they invariably consisted of "public events at which opponents prostrated themselves before the ruler and begged for forgiveness."[38] But rulers also performed angry scenes, even though anger was not praised in the advice books. Already J. E. A. Jolliffe had spoken of royal anger as a regular part of medieval English governance. For Althoff the matter was more complex. Even ideal rulership required "compulsion and fear." But moralists' attitudes toward royal anger per se were not static, and therefore neither were representations of the angry king. In the twelfth century – precisely the period Jolliffe wrote about – royal anger found its justification in theory: the king's "righteous" anger was treated as a form of justice.[39] In accord with medieval moralist teaching, then, medieval performances of emotion were well controlled. They were, in a word, "rituals." Because of this, Althoff's approach meshed very well with some of the studies of medieval rituals that were underway around the same time, such as Geoffrey Koziol's consideration of the practices of begging favor and pardon.[40]

Althoff's use of "performance" to explain the rational – often political – significance of emotional displays influenced many historians, especially medievalists. It was particularly helpful to those who studied the so-called "theater-state" of Burgundy. An ephemeral creation that lasted a bit more than a century (1364 to 1482), Burgundy was the work of dukes descended from the French royal house. Taking advantage of the chaos of the Hundred Years' War between England and France, they carved out an independent polity that ran from north to south and included regions with disparate traditions and affiliations. The dukes held their state together with rituals – of entry, exit, travel, warfare, peacemaking, marriages, banqueting, entertaining and emotional display. Thus, Klaus Oschema studied friendships and alliances in the Duchy of Burgundy as examples of the "staging" of emotions – emotional displays that were tantamount to "institutions." This formulation did not deny their emotional meaning, just as the modern signature on a marriage contract does not disaffirm a couple's love. The difference between the rituals of the past and now turns on the centrality of the body: in the Middle Ages, the physical ruler was the instrument of emotional *and* political expression. Even though the Burgundian state drew up plenty of written documents, "when we observe the peace agreements and treaties of the period, what strikes us are the references to love and friendship as well as the awareness and the use of the bodies of the political protagonists."[41]

More recently, Laurent Smagghe opened wide the political vistas by considering *all* the "emotions of the prince." He noted that the Burgundian sources treated emotions in two ways: if feelings were expressed properly, they followed "implicit stage directions that gave spiritual and moral ballast to the effectiveness of [governmental] power"; if expressed inopportunely, they were the basis of moral judgments by observers, who also supplied a barrage of edifying contrary examples. Smagghe proposed to show which emotions worked to the advantage of the prince and which did not. He began with the body, movement, and *habitus* (a term used by Pierre Bourdieu to indicate social practices that were internalized and carried out – often slightly sabotaged or at least improvised – by individuals within that culture). Smagghe continued his discussion by considering princely shows of anger, laughter, and tears.[42]

Historians have not confined their use of the performative approach to the Middle Ages. Classicists have looked at the ways in which emotions figured in Greek and Roman oratory. For the modern world, Doris Kolesch has fruitfully studied the emotions expressed at the court of Louis XIV. While both Elias and Reddy considered that court to be an engine of emotional repression, Kolesch dubbed it a "society of pleasure," citing its many venues for feeling: its spectacles, feasts, gardens, amusements. Louis' court was suffused with a pervasive "courtly emotionality," an aesthetics of passion that took its tone from the theater of life as well as of the stage.[43]

The performative approach does not deny that people may feel the emotions that they display, nor (on the other hand) does it deny that they may feign their emotions. Its emphasis is on the external effects of emotions as they play out in front of others, and also on the ways in which those effects, whether desired or dreaded, define the self who is emoting. In short, it is concerned above all with the body.

Approaches applied: The Declaration of Independence of the United States

It is useful to ask how these four different approaches to the history of emotions might work when confronting the same text: The Declaration of Independence. Of course, we are speculating here, trying to apply techniques that were for the most part never brought to bear on this specific text. But the exercise is useful to highlight the differences as well as the similarities among theories by means of very brief sketches of the possibilities.

The Declaration was written by Thomas Jefferson (d.1826) in 1776. It is perhaps not an obvious candidate for a discussion of emotions; some would say it is not very "emotional." Yet there are at least three reasons why this possible objection should not hold. First, coming at any document with a preconceived idea of what is "emotional" is not the best historical method. Second, a list of grievances may be exactly the sort of thing to both express and arouse emotions. Third, the Declaration includes at least one word that is today ordinarily considered an emotion: "happiness."

Transcription of the Declaration of Independence

In Congress, July 4, 1776.

The unanimous Declaration of the thirteen united States of America,
When in the Course of human events, it becomes necessary for one people
to dissolve the political bands which have connected them with another,
and to assume among the powers of the earth, the separate and equal
station to which the Laws of Nature and of Nature's God entitle them,
a decent respect to the opinions of mankind requires that they should
declare the causes which impel them to the separation.

We hold these truths to be self-evident, that all men are created equal,
that they are endowed by their Creator with certain unalienable Rights,
that among these are Life, Liberty and the pursuit of Happiness. – That
to secure these rights, Governments are instituted among Men, deriving
their just powers from the consent of the governed, – That whenever
any Form of Government becomes destructive of these ends, it is the
Right of the People to alter or to abolish it, and to institute new Government, laying its foundation on such principles and organizing its powers
in such form, as to them shall seem most likely to effect their Safety
and Happiness. Prudence, indeed, will dictate that Governments long
established should not be changed for light and transient causes; and
accordingly all experience hath shewn, that mankind are more disposed
to suffer, while evils are sufferable, than to right themselves by abolishing the forms to which they are accustomed. But when a long train of
abuses and usurpations, pursuing invariably the same Object evinces a
design to reduce them under absolute Despotism, it is their right, it is
their duty, to throw off such Government, and to provide new Guards
for their future security. – Such has been the patient sufferance of these
Colonies; and such is now the necessity which constrains them to alter
their former Systems of Government. The history of the present King
of Great Britain is a history of repeated injuries and usurpations, all
having in direct object the establishment of an absolute Tyranny over
these States. To prove this, let Facts be submitted to a candid world.

He has refused his Assent to Laws, the most wholesome and necessary
for the public good.

He has forbidden his Governors to pass Laws of immediate and pressing
importance, unless suspended in their operation till his Assent should
be obtained; and when so suspended, he has utterly neglected to attend
to them.

He has refused to pass other Laws for the accommodation of large districts
of people, unless those people would relinquish the right of Representation
in the Legislature, a right inestimable to them and formidable to tyrants
only.

He has called together legislative bodies at places unusual, uncomfortable, and distant from the depository of their public Records, for the sole purpose of fatiguing them into compliance with his measures.

He has dissolved Representative Houses repeatedly, for opposing with manly firmness his invasions on the rights of the people.

He has refused for a long time, after such dissolutions, to cause others to be elected; whereby the Legislative powers, incapable of Annihilation, have returned to the People at large for their exercise; the State remaining in the mean time exposed to all the dangers of invasion from without, and convulsions within.

He has endeavoured to prevent the population of these States; for that purpose obstructing the Laws for Naturalization of Foreigners; refusing to pass others to encourage their migrations hither, and raising the conditions of new Appropriations of Lands.

He has obstructed the Administration of Justice, by refusing his Assent to Laws for establishing Judiciary powers.

He has made Judges dependent on his Will alone, for the tenure of their offices, and the amount and payment of their salaries.

He has erected a multitude of New Offices, and sent hither swarms of Officers to harrass our people, and eat out their substance.

He has kept among us, in times of peace, Standing Armies without the Consent of our legislatures.

He has affected to render the Military independent of and superior to the Civil power.

He has combined with others to subject us to a jurisdiction foreign to our constitution, and unacknowledged by our laws; giving his Assent to their Acts of pretended Legislation:

For Quartering large bodies of armed troops among us:

For protecting them, by a mock Trial, from punishment for any Murders which they should commit on the Inhabitants of these States:

For cutting off our Trade with all parts of the world:

For imposing Taxes on us without our Consent:

For depriving us in many cases, of the benefits of Trial by Jury:

For transporting us beyond Seas to be tried for pretended offences:

For abolishing the free System of English Laws in a neighbouring Province, establishing therein an Arbitrary government, and enlarging its Boundaries so as to render it at once an example and fit instrument for introducing the same absolute rule into these Colonies:

For taking away our Charters, abolishing our most valuable Laws, and altering fundamentally the Forms of our Governments:

For suspending our own Legislatures, and declaring themselves invested with power to legislate for us in all cases whatsoever.

He has abdicated Government here, by declaring us out of his Protection and waging War against us.

He has plundered our seas, ravaged our Coasts, burnt our towns, and destroyed the lives of our people.

He is at this time transporting large Armies of foreign Mercenaries to compleat the works of death, desolation and tyranny, already begun with circumstances of Cruelty & perfidy scarcely paralleled in the most barbarous ages, and totally unworthy the Head of a civilized nation.

He has constrained our fellow Citizens taken Captive on the high Seas to bear Arms against their Country, to become the executioners of their friends and Brethren, or to fall themselves by their Hands.

He has excited domestic insurrections amongst us, and has endeavoured to bring on the inhabitants of our frontiers, the merciless Indian Savages, whose known rule of warfare, is an undistinguished destruction of all ages, sexes and conditions.

In every stage of these Oppressions We have Petitioned for Redress in the most humble terms: Our repeated Petitions have been answered only by repeated injury. A Prince whose character is thus marked by every act which may define a Tyrant, is unfit to be the ruler of a free people.

Nor have We been wanting in attentions to our British brethren. We have warned them from time to time of attempts by their legislature to extend an unwarrantable jurisdiction over us. We have reminded them of the circumstances of our emigration and settlement here. We have appealed to their native justice and magnanimity, and we have conjured them by the ties of our common kindred to disavow these usurpations, which, would inevitably interrupt our connections and correspondence. They too have been deaf to the voice of justice and of consanguinity. We must, therefore, acquiesce in the necessity, which denounces our Separation, and hold them, as we hold the rest of mankind, Enemies in War, in Peace Friends.

We, therefore, the Representatives of the united States of America, in General Congress, Assembled, appealing to the Supreme Judge of the world for the rectitude of our intentions, do, in the Name, and by Authority of the good People of these Colonies, solemnly publish and declare, That these United Colonies are, and of Right ought to be Free and Independent States; that they are Absolved from all Allegiance to the British Crown, and that all political connection between them and the State of Great Britain, is and ought to be totally dissolved; and that as Free and Independent States, they have full Power to levy War, conclude Peace, contract Alliances, establish Commerce, and to do all other Acts and Things which Independent States may of right do. And for the support of this Declaration, with a firm reliance on the protection of divine Providence, we mutually pledge to each other our Lives, our Fortunes and our sacred Honor.

[Signatures follow]

Source: https://www.archives.gov/founding-docs/declaration-transcript

Emotionology

With its emphasis on basic emotions and changing standards regarding them, emotionology requires us to ask what standards of happiness had been absorbed by American colonists by the time the Declaration was written. It stands to reason that those standards would find their way into public policy – even into the Declaration. There were no advice books for the middle class – indeed, there was not much of a middle class at all – in the period. Nevertheless, there were "conduct books." C. Dallett Hemphill found that around the mid eighteenth century the monopoly of traditional conduct books, which dated all the way back to the Renaissance and were read only by the elite, was ending. Coming on the market were new conduct books written for "a broader group of prosperous Anglo-American families." The emphasis of these manuals was on "control of the body and face," the face above all. "One was to appear 'easy and affable' and to strike a balance between formality and familiarity." By far the most popular guide was Lord Chesterfield's *Letters to His Son*. "Chesterfield recommended 'a certain degree of outward seriousness ... and decent cheerfulness' in one's 'looks.'" Advice books for women told them much the same thing: their speech, behavior, and faces were to be "cheerful and gay, but with just the right amount of modest reserve to awe men into proper behavior."[44]

Picking up on this point, Stearns himself considered the implications of Chesterfield's advice for the Declaration of Independence:

> The push toward happiness, a major change in Western culture, stemmed in part from new intellectual impulses – including a greater philosophical acceptance of material progress – but it seemed to nestle compatibly enough with the first phases of modernity. In contrast to centuries in which people had been urged to humility before God, amid considerable valuation of a slightly melancholic personal presentation, a new chorus of advice urged not only the validity but the social importance of cheerfulness. The idea caught on rapidly enough that upstart Americans even included a right to happiness in their revolutionary documentation.

Here Stearns argued that the validation of happiness went hand-in-hand with the rejection of the sober religious outlook beloved in Calvinism. It was a pivotal moment: modernity – with its celebration of steam-driven factories, its Enlightenment faith in human ingenuity, its acceptance of worldly ambition, its pursuit of wealth and comfort – made cheerfulness not simply acceptable but a requisite virtue. When yellow fever broke out in Philadelphia, Stearns noted, the reaction was not to bewail human sin or give way to grief but rather to tell people "to keep up their spirits." That new attitude was already clear in the Declaration.[45]

Emotional regimes

Reddy's approach does not postulate basic emotions or put stress on particular "emotion words" like happiness. Rather, he is interested in the ways in which a given situation allows – or does not allow – for emotional self-alteration and exploration. The document then, per se, is not so important. It is tempting to imagine that, from the point of view of emotives and emotional regimes, the American Revolution was a dress-rehearsal for the French. But this is too simple. As Nicole Eustace shows, American Revolutionary authors were inspired by sentimentalism, but, in America, this was not a refuge. To the contrary, in America sentimentalism was the emotional regime. It ratified the status quo.

In the colonies, Eustace points out, emotions were as much markers of status as of feeling. Although elite colonial men addressed business associates with terms of endearment, they never used such vocabulary with their servants or slaves. If they got angry, they made sure to express it with due restraint; only low-ranking people would let anger overwhelm them (or so the thinking went). The elites in colonial New England cultivated the genteel feelings that, in their view, put them on the same level as the English elites. They thought that the emotions of others – black slaves, poor whites, women – were "alternately inadequate and excessive."

Where, then, was the colonial emotional refuge? It was perhaps with people like Thomas Paine, who "insisted that the propensity for passion was universal – inevitable, invariable, and even desirable in all people." Or perhaps it was to be found in the rhetoric of grief that the colonists adopted around the time of the Stamp Act Congress in 1765. As Eustace put it, "grief backed up by anger could convey resistance in respectful terms while heading off any imputations of weakness." Mourning became a "mode of protest."[46] In that sense, happiness was the emotion – or, rather, in the lingo of the time, the "passion" – that countered the sorrow the colonists felt under the British. Either way, the Declaration of Independence signaled the triumph of the refuge, but its idea of equality and freedom applied only to white males. The "pursuit of happiness" in the Declaration was just another privilege for the sorts of men who drafted and signed it and who would form the new regime. The legacy of that elitism remains with us today.

Emotional communities

The first task of a researcher wanting to understand the Declaration from the point of view of emotional communities is to note who signed the document. The second task is to gather a dossier of writings by those men (for they were all men) and to analyze it for its emotions. What did "happiness" mean to the signatories? Did they belong to one emotional community – or more than one?

Jan Lewis has explored the world of Jefferson and made some pertinent observations in this regard. In eighteenth-century Virginia happiness was the feeling that followed from independence. "If I was independent," wrote one young man, "I should be happy." What did independence mean, exactly? According to Lewis, a happy man was one free of "entangling relationships with others and especially from debt." Only in the nineteenth century did happiness come to be connected to private satisfactions rather than public status. In this light, the Declaration's evocation of "happiness" referred to a proud personal independence, another facet of "liberty," while its emphasis on "pursuit" emphasized the "steadiness of mind, and evenness of manners," that was thought to bring "Happiness in Life."[47]

That was its meaning in one emotional community. But while happiness may have meant that to the Virginian Jefferson, it appears to have meant something rather different to those living in Philadelphia. There (where the Declaration was signed), educated colonists eagerly absorbed the *Essay on Man*, published between 1732 and 1738 by English poet Alexander Pope. As Eustace has shown, Pope argued that passions – we would say "emotions" – were essential "to advance self and society simultaneously."[48] When Pope wrote his poetic *Essay*, he was already well known as a translator of Homer. His Greek was excellent, and he knew very well, from Aristotle, that *eudaimonia* – i.e. happiness, well-being – was the end, that is, the goal, of man. It meant acting in accordance with virtue. Striving toward this goal depended, according to Aristotle, on all the things commonly thought necessary for the good life: beauty, health, wealth, power. In part, these things came from human effort and in part from good fortune. When Pope wrote that happiness is "our being's end and aim!," he was properly translating Aristotle.[49] As Phil Withington has shown, when "happiness" entered the English language in the mid fifteenth century, "it derived from the Old Norse noun, 'hap,' meaning luck or fortune."[50] That was close enough to *eudaimonia* for Pope to use it in his translation.

But Pope also used happiness in a Christian context, in which the highest good was not in this life. Thus, according to Pope, happiness is that "which prompts the eternal sigh,/ For which we bear to live, or dare to die, which still so near us, yet beyond us lies." We "sigh" for it; we "dare to die" for it. In short, we "pursue" it. If Pope was on the minds of some of the signatories of the Declaration, as he probably was, this may have been how they understood it. And they may have seen Pope's sort of happiness as a further elaboration of "All men are created equal." In Pope's poetry, happiness did not mean that there should be no status differences, for "Order is Heaven's first law; and this confest [confessed],/ Some are, and must be, greater than the rest." Happiness for Pope was not individual felicity but rather a quality of the community as a whole: "Remember, man, 'the Universal Cause/ Acts not by partial, but by general laws;'/ And makes what happiness we justly call subsist not in the good of one, but all." In the emotional communities of Virginians and Philadelphians in 1776, the first meaning of happiness was not exactly "cheerfulness," but it certainly was the opposite of that "rhetoric of mournfulness" that colonists had begun to cultivate at the time of the Stamp Act.

Performatives

How can there be a "performative" approach to a document when performatives are so utterly linked to the body and its gestures? The answer is that written materials, too, have a body, an appearance. They too *present* themselves; the very "look" of the Declaration of Independence announces its importance (see Plate 4). It is large (about 24 inches x 30 inches); it uses many different forms of script to telegraph its authority and to make clear its various sections; its layout is deliberate, its separate points delineated by lines; it is written on parchment, though not "a particularly good sheet... just an ordinary type of colonial manufacture." In the 1920s, it was exhibited at the Library of Congress as if within a shrine, framed and made to stand upright like an altarpiece. Today it sits in state, protected by an airtight container, in the Rotunda of the National Archives Building, next to the United States Constitution. Abraham Lincoln appealed to its authority to condemn slavery; Martin Luther King invoked it as "a promissory note to which every American was to fall heir ... that all men, yes, black men as well as white men, would be guaranteed the unalienable rights of life, liberty, and the pursuit of happiness." Like one of Althoff's kings, or Hochschild's stewardesses, it was groomed to make statements.[51]

The Declaration performed as well in its original historical context. People at the time would have been familiar with royal decrees from the King of Great Britain. These had the same "look," a design that dated back to the medieval period and, indeed, the ancient world. The colonists were used to language about rights, which dated back to the twelfth century, when Church law talked about "the rights of liberty," the "right of the power to elect," and elaborated on the idea of natural rights. The works of John Locke (d.1704) on government – of enormous influence in the American colonies – spoke of men's equality and the preciousness of their "life, health, liberty, [and] possessions," in short, their "rights."

Royal documents on behalf of the colonists often included clauses about "rights," as did the documents drafted by the colonists themselves.[52]

The Declaration's words are also performative. They create a new and independent state and name the very people involved in that creation. Moreover, the names are in the form of personal signatures: the Declaration thereby takes on legal force, obligating the signatories to a future course of action. At the same time, it evokes past actions: real people took up pens, perhaps hesitated for a moment or, like John Hancock, proudly wrote their names with a flourish. The physical look of the Declaration conjures up a moment that is reimagined every time it is read. That is the performative context in which the pursuit of happiness must be read: each clause about the injustices of the king *performs* that very pursuit as it declares the acts of the Crown illegitimate.

So far, the performance seems less emotional than political: the document asserts its own authority. But recall that for Althoff, emotions were above all communicative modes – political statements in the form of gestures. Was the Declaration such for the men signing it? From Philadelphia, on July 1, 1776, Jefferson wrote to William Fleming (former governor of Virginia) about his anxieties: he was 300 miles away from his home,

> and thereby open to secret assassination without a possibility of self-defence. I am willing to hope nothing of this kind has been done in my case, and yet I cannot be easy. If any doubt has arisen as to me, my country will have my political creed in the form of a 'Declaration &c.' which I was lately directed to draw. This will give decisive proof that my own sentiment concurred with the vote they instructed us to give.[53]

So for Jefferson, the Declaration was a gesture of solidarity with "his country" even unto death. Another signer, John Adams, writing at the same time to Samuel Chase (a representative from Maryland), was equally worried:

> If you imagine that I expect this Declaration, will ward off, Calamities from this Country, you are much mistaken. A bloody Conflict We are destined to endure. ... If you imagine that I flatter myself with

Happiness and Halcyon days, after a Seperation from Great Britain
ꞏꞏꞏꞏ ꞏꞏꞏ ꞏꞏꞏꞏꞏꞏꞏꞏꞏ ꞏꞏꞏꞏꞏ

He fortified himself with the thought that "Freedom is a Counterballance for Poverty, Discord, and War, and more."[54] Here the Declaration functioned as a statement of priorities that, in part, rejected easy feelings.

Disparities

These approaches yield different results. Some researchers will no doubt want to put them together in a kind of "bricolage." Before they do so, some caveats are in order. The approaches are different for good reason. They rest on disparate foundations that make them, if not entirely compatible, then at least not entirely complementary.

Emotionology is interested above all in modernity. That is why Stearns starts with modern conceptions, emotions, and emotion words. He looks at how attitudes toward them have changed because he wants to understand the private lives and public policies of today. Reddy is more interested in the human condition – we are born with emotives (which demand that we change) but fated to live with emotional regimes (which demand that we conform). His scheme allows him to critique Western society and its emotional traditions, yet at the same time, it recognizes that those traditions are bound to alter as regimes and refuges succeed one another. Rosenwein, by contrast with both, is concerned with variety. Her technique is microhistorical: she assumes that looking at specific groups will yield the most telling insights about the larger whole. She thinks that people are born into – or carve out, or find – emotional communities in which they feel comfortable, at least for the most part. She argues that many different emotional communities co-exist at the same time. The performative view begins with the body – its gestures, its pronouncements. It does not deny that people may feel their emotions, but that is not its main concern. It treats the world as a stage.

These approaches evaluate theories of emotions differently. Stearns accepts modern theories of basic emotions, and he sees the emotion theories of the past as helping to steer emotionology. They enter into advice books; they guide people as they control the expression of their emotions. In Reddy's case, some modern scientific theories suggest the idea of emotives, but his understanding of them is entirely his own. He is not particularly interested in past theories. For Rosenwein, both past and modern theories are important. The latter support in part her view that vocabularies of emotion are key. The former help explain those very vocabularies. Althoff is not concerned with theories of emotion; rather, he cares about modes of communication.

The four approaches also have different expectations about emotional change. Emotionology assumes that emotional categories – anger, fear, love, and so on – are stable, while standards regarding them change continually. Emotives, on the other hand, postulate that emotions are in constant flux: to pin an emotion down would be to take away its liberty. Less labile are the emotions of Rosenwein's communities. Each community has its own emotional vocabulary, which is fairly stable for a while. Normally this vocabulary is more or less shared with other contemporary communities, as when both Puritans and Levellers reveled in the idea of freedom. They understood one another. But, even so, they did not agree on what constituted freedom. As for the performative view, it requires emotions to have fixed meanings since their function is to signal certain well-understood messages to a public, whether large or small.

Finally, the approaches differ regarding "emotion management." Emotionology posits that people want to manage their emotions "properly," but it takes about a generation for a new emotionology to be fully absorbed and implemented. For Reddy, the existence of emotives makes all emotional control a form of labor, a "domain of effort." Emotional regimes demand this labor, which is necessary to preserve political and social stability. But controlling emotions always involves struggling against the very nature of emotives. Rosenwein admits that Western theories of emotions stress their management. But the very multiplicity of emotional communities means that people have some choices. Thus, as she puts it, "On the ground, ... emotional communities do not seem to struggle with the effort to control their emotions. ... Furthermore, emotional communities seem to relish their emotional norms and values."[55] The performative view makes emotional labor conform to rules and social needs that make up larger systems of political and social practice.

Few historians (apart from Stearns, Reddy, Rosenwein, and Althoff, of course) would ally themselves categorically with one or another approach. Many, indeed, work on specific aspects or topics that may seem at first glance unrelated to any of these methodologies. Yet, much of the newer work in the field does have a family resemblance, putting great emphasis on bodies. The many ways in which these studies understand the body and the emotions is the subject of Chapter 3.

3
Bodies

"The things we call the parts in every living being are so inseparable from the whole that they may be understood only in and with the whole."

Goethe, "A Study based on Spinoza" (*c.*1785)

Since the early twenty-first century, historians of emotions have combined the "foundational approaches" explored in Chapters 1 and 2 with new interests that, however disparate they may seem at first, have the body as their overarching theme. Nevertheless, they see the body in two quite distinct ways. In one, it is bounded and autonomous, and everything emotionally significant goes on *within* it. Emotions are physiological, connected to the brain, guts, and heart. In the second, the body is porous and merges with its environment. It is defined by space, architectures, and the objects around it; it is in effect part of the material world. These visions are, however, somewhat artificial, as few thinkers want to argue that the body is either entirely autonomous or utterly permeable. Indeed, as we shall see, both practice theory and affect theory to some degree straddle the two kinds of bodies.

If these different approaches to the body seem bewildering, readers should be encouraged by the fact that this is nothing new. Already in 1995, Caroline Bynum was complaining that current discussions of the body were "almost completely incommensurate – and often mutually incomprehensible – across the disciplines." She was referring to scholarly works in which the body was basically either "natural" (the physiological approach) or "cultural" (the social constructionist view). Is the recent history of the emotions reconciling this opposition? Is the new focus on emotions helping to write a more complete and nuanced body history? Scrutinizing the most recent literature on the body, we realized how much medicine, suffering, pain, gender, and so forth, still attract historians. But how is the new focus on the *emotional body* reshaping those topics?[1]

The bounded body

In 1974, when Jacques Le Goff and Pierre Nora edited a manifesto calling for "new directions in history," the subtitle for their only chapter on the body was "the ill person in history." Indeed, interest in the body – a largely autonomous "scientific body" – was at first driven by histories of medicine and hygiene. Though emotions were not yet a focus, that same chapter also (if briefly) noted that the body was the place of desire and pain – i.e. of emotion. Following the appearance of that influential book, historical scholarship on the body focused on malady and suffering.[2]

Initially, both gender and sexuality were also treated as issues of the bounded, medicalized body. For instance, Danielle Jacquart and Claude Thomasset studied sexuality and medicine in the Middle Ages, and Thomas Laqueur looked at developments in reproductive anatomy and physiology to tell the story of sex from the Greeks to Freud. Even Michel Foucault – despite his criticism of viewing the body as merely a "locus of physiological processes and metabolisms" or a "target for the attacks of germs or viruses" – resorted to the history of medical knowledge to understand the context in which "medicine framed the question of sexual pleasures."[3]

Historians of emotions and gender, too, initially accepted a physical definition of their topic, seeing gender as a matter of male and female sex organs. That, however, changed, as the idea of gender as a social performance took hold. In the wake of social constructionist ideas, *à la* Foucault, historians like Peter Brown and Caroline Walker Bynum made the uses of the body contingent on the ambient context. Brown studied the celibate body in early Christianity, a body shaped by social and religious groups that highly valued the life-long renunciation of all sexual activity. For her part, Bynum studied the ecstatic, starving body of women in late medieval Europe to illuminate the nature both of their piety and of the religious sensibilities of their fellow Christians. Celibacy and starving are, from one point of view, "practices of the body." Reminiscent of Marcel Mauss' "techniques of the body" – the different ways various societies taught people to "use their bodies" – such practices have motivated historians of emotions to elaborate on what we are here calling "the practiced body." As historians of emotions turned to this topic – how bodies move, and how those movements both express and generate emotions – they made much of the ways in which the body and the world interacted together. Here we come close to the idea of the porous body.[4]

The physiological body

The connections between emotions and medicine emerged as a fruitful field of study already in the 1990s. It was then that historian Otniel Dror (who also trained as a physician) wrote about the rise of a new, laboratory-based science of emotion beginning in the late nineteenth and early twentieth centuries. Physiologists, psychologists, and medical profession-als made the body – unrelated to mind or soul – the key to emotions. They championed physiological tests to isolate and explore the nature of fear, laughter, and surprise, inventing emotion-gauging technologies to record bodily states: meta-bolic rates, blood pressures, body-heat regulations, cardiac rhythms, intestinal contractions, and so on. Victorian scientists had evaluated emotions qualitatively. The new physiologists, psychologists, and clinicians insisted on objective measures that could be represented in numbers and graphs. Their definition of "normal" was not the body in its habitual, emotionally laden state within a social context, but rather the *non*-emotional body in the laboratory. The body was transparent, "speaking" to the researcher through impartial instruments, regardless of what the patient said, willed, or knew. The implications of this view were vast. Machines like lie detectors were said to get at the truth; indeed, they alone were deemed capable of delving into the true self.[5]

Dror reviewed a significant aspect of this new approach to the emotions by contrasting it with Foucault's notion of "examination." For Foucault, "the examination is at the centre of the procedures that constitute the individual as effect and object of power." Foucault spoke of the "medical gaze" that alienated the person from her body. Citing the Panopticon – the eighteenth-century "model" prison that allowed every prisoner to be observed at all times by a single watchman – Foucault asserted that "he who is subjected to a field of visibility, and who knows it, assumes responsibility for the constraints of power." In other words, the subject allows himself to be manipulated, accepting the judgment and the purposes of those who gaze. For Foucault, the gaze disciplined the body. For Dror's scientists, however, the examination did the opposite: it activated certain uncontrollable emotional dynamics. These the scientists measured, even while considering them manifestations of the "transient and 'phantom' body." The "real," the "normal," they thought, ironically, was "the de-emotionalized, 'anesthetized' body."[6]

While Dror looked at how post-Victorian doctors emotionalized the body, examining blood pressure, skin temperature, hormonal systems, and so on to discover the nature of emotions, Fay Bound Alberti looked at an earlier period, when physicians theorized the body more holistically. In a collection of essays published in 2006, she and her collaborators explored ideas about emotions prevalent in the seventeenth and eighteenth centuries, before the rise of laboratory medicine, when physicians assumed that the emotions of the body were enmeshed in "the mind/body/soul relation." Only the gradual demotion of this view made possible the later scientific focus on "the brain and the central nervous system" of our own day and the rise of psychiatrists, neuroscientists, and psychologists as professional specialists of emotions as mental phenomena.[7]

Bound Alberti pursued this theme further in her 2010 study of the heart, long considered the seat and very symbol of emotion. Studying the origins – both spiritual and cultural – of this view of the heart, she traced its beginnings in classical Greece, its crystallization in the writings of Galen (d.210), and its persistence in medical training over the course of millennia. The heart was at the very center of the mind/body/ soul complex, "affected by the operations of the soul" and affecting in turn the mind and body. Even when the heart gained new identity "merely as a pump" in the seventeenth century, physicians did not cease to stress its pivotal role in the production of emotions "capable of causing profound structural changes in the body, and in the mind." Bound Alberti considered "angina pectoris," a cardiac disease newly "discovered" in the late eighteenth century. Today, the American Heart Association has a straightforward mechanical explanation for the disease: "It occurs when the heart muscle doesn't get as much blood as it needs ... [usually] because one or more of the heart's arteries is narrowed or blocked." But when angina pectoris was first defined, it was deemed "as much a product of emotional distress as structural disease." That explains why colleagues of surgeon and anatomist John Hunter blamed his death from angina pectoris in 1793 as much on his "irascibility" as on physical factors. In Hunter's day "the heart remained an organ of emotion as well as the body. ... The mind and body were linked, a position made possible by nervous physiology that united the experiences of each through the doctrines and notions of sensibility and sympathy."[8]

From the nineteenth century onward, however, the heart gave way to the brain as the seat of emotions in scientific thought. But in the process, the heart's "status as a cultural artefact" (as Bound Alberti put it) "became paradoxically more emotional: the feeling heart was crucial to the Romantic project and provided evidence of creativity and the divine." Bound Alberti is critical of the Western disconnect between what the modern scientific community says about the heart and the embedded cultural traditions that even today inspire us to acknowledge the unity of mind and body. Scientists have largely failed to put pumps and valentines together. Nevertheless, as Bound Alberti notes, very recently physicians have begun to add some "romance" to their explorations. She points to new research on "cellular memories" and pathways of "neurons and synapses" in the heart "akin to those that exist in the brain." Since her book on the heart was published, scientists have even more recently argued that grief and stress produce cardiomyopathy. In her most recent book, which looks at the whole body, from inner guts to outer skin. Bound Alberti discusses how every element of human physiology, both today and in the past, has participated in both "our emotions and our rational appetites."[9]

Elena Carrera took up a similar theme in her exploration of "prescriptive and descriptive discussions of emotions in the context of medical advice circulating in Europe between 1200 and 1700." Wishing to fill the chronological gap left by Rosenwein's and Reddy's first books on the history of emotions, Carrera criticized Rosenwein for the narrowness of "emotional communities," and urged a wider, more all-inclusive view. Her aim was "to show the continuity of ideas on the interaction of body and mind, and on the embodied soul as a purposeful composite, across a wide range of cultural discourses." Thus, while acknowledging the cultural specificity of emotions as reflected in the changing words and lexicons of various communities, Carrera stressed the longevity of the emotions that were connected to long-term goals and cross-cultural values, like health, or well-being. The persistence of such commonalities made Carrera insist on far more capacious and long-lasting emotional communities than Rosenwein had envisioned. Indeed, Carrera suggested that they might better be termed "trans-historical ideological groups."[10]

But were notions of well-being as durable as Carrera imagined? While today well-being is antithetical to pain and suffering, this was not always the case. As scholars have probed the meaning of pain, particularly in the Christian West, they have discovered that it, too, was a welcome part of some definitions of the good life. Christian religious discourse made pain and suffering desirable because they recalled and imitated the grieving body of Christ. The full implications of this insight have yet to be exhausted. Already in 2005 Jacques Gélis's contribution to an influential three-volume *Histoire du corps* made the point: "To become Christ's body, to pass through all of the trials suffered by the Man of Sorrows: that is the highest aspiration." Gélis was talking about the time span from the Renaissance to the Enlightenment. The assertion was made even more strongly by Jan Frans van Dijkhuizen and Karl A. E. Enenkel in a collection of articles on the somewhat longer period between 1300 and 1700. In their words, that era "witnessed something like a *theological pain contest.*" While Protestantism denied the usefulness of pain for men's salvation, the Counter Reformation "intensified the cultivation of physical suffering that had also characterized late medieval Catholicism."[11]

Two years after van Dijkhuizen and Enenkel's anthology appeared, Esther Cohen's *The Modulated Scream* looked at the late Middle Ages, where various intellectual communities (legal thinkers, medical specialists, theologians) had much to say in favor of pain. Mystics and penitents sought to suffer in imitation of Christ, while medieval judges considered pain and torture essential tools for extracting truth. Far from mitigating pain, physicians relied on it to locate the sites and sources of diseases. The Christian religion itself understood the pains of Hell as part of God's plan. In the fourteenth and fifteenth centuries, people gave voice to pain: they were expected to scream, and they did so.[12]

In their recent book on the history of emotions during the entire medieval period in the West, Damien Boquet and Piroska Nagy make pain – and, more precisely, the suffering body of Christ – the stable element of an otherwise changing emotional landscape. Beginning with the "Christianization of emotions," their book continues with monastic communities that institutionalized what Jean Leclercq famously termed "the desire for God." Monks exercised the right emotions in the right ways and for the right purposes. Soon, the authors show, the practices of the monastery opened out to the rest of society at large, creating "a Christian society" that was continually infused over the course of time by the values and emotions of newly invigorated religious groups, such as the twelfth-century hermits and the ecclesiastical courtiers who surrounded the German emperor. A sort of call and response among lay aristocrats and princes, town citizens, and specialists of prayer, theology, and medicine allowed for enriched emotional possibilities. Emotions are, in this book, sometimes treated as standards, sometimes as elements of emotional regimes or communities, often as performatives. At all times, for Boquet and Nagy, new interpretations of Christ's pain and love shaped medieval emotions.[13]

The Christian tradition made pain both physical and cultural. That synthesis is rare today, but the essays in van Dijkhuizen and Enenkel's collection argue that it was quite normal in

the early modern period, even apart from the strictly Christian tradition Michael Schoenfeldt argues, for example, that
"much of the immense attraction of Stoicism in the period
derived from the fact that it offered a philosophical strategy for dealing with the inevitable onslaught of physical
and emotional suffering." Pain and its interpretation went
together.[14]

Cultural historian Joanna Bourke makes this a general
axiom. As she says, "the body is never pure soma: it is con-
figured in social, cognitive, and metaphorical worlds." She
finds a way around the mind–body dualism by conceptualizing
pain as a "type of event," as a "way-of-being in the world."
The meanings of such pain events changed historically. "From
the moment of birth, infants are initiated into cultures of pain.
What these infants in the 1760s learnt about the cognitive,
affective, and sensory meanings arising from the interface
between their interior bodies and the external world was very
different to what their counterparts in the 1960s learnt." What
they learned was, often, political, for learning is determined
by those in power, whether parents or rulers. Even the names
of various pains, says Bourke, lay bare the exercise of power.
Today "hunger," for instance, is less serious than "being in
terrible pain," and it calls forth less sympathy, less money,
and less social organization.[15]

Javier Moscoso, too, has tracked the cultural forms that
the experience of pain – physiological pain and its subjective
expression – has taken in the last five centuries. Like so many
other approaches connected with the body, Moscoso's is performative. He affirms that "pain exists under the form of a
social drama," and it is directly through this theatricality, in
the guise of "commonplaces" (like "representation," "imitation," "sympathy" etc.), that Moscoso seeks to analyze the
"intersubjective" reality of pain. By *intersubjective* he means
the ways in which our experiences – past and present, along
with their sensory and emotional associations – are fused
together in any one moment. The likelihood that the experience
of pain "will be culturally meaningful increases depending on
whether it can be imitated or represented." In the end, pain
might – as Elaine Scarry thought in 1985 – resist language,
but it always welcomes modes of interpretation, modes that
are commonplace but nonetheless "persuasive."[16]

In an anthology edited by Rob Boddice that explicitly ties pain to emotions, pain is like an emotive: when the bodily experience of pain is "translate[d] into words, grimaces, and art, ... we literally 'figure out' what we feel." Just as the emotive transforms the one emoting, so too it alters its audience. For Boddice, pain and emotion are one and the same: both are "feelings" felt in the body but "translated" into utterances. Gone here entirely is Scarry's notion of pain's voiceless essence, and pain's domain is extended "from the operating theatre or clinical office to the waiting room; from the moment of birth to its anticipation and its aftermath... [it includes] grief, anxiety, depression, hysteria, nervousness, despair and other 'mental illnesses.' " Modifying Aristotle, who made pain accompany emotion, Boddice has emotions accompany pain: "physical pain is not meaningful without ... some other affective component (even pleasure, joy or ecstasy)." It stands to reason, then, that pain is part of every emotional regime: "the question of whose pain is *authentic* is a question of power." Indeed, physicians should rethink the questions they ask about pain, for pain's political role is "ever-present and always to someone's disadvantage." A good example is "phantom pain," which doctors cannot explain and so is called "phantom" even as it gives pain. "Pain rules," like "emotion rules," produce emotional suffering – in other words, pain![17]

The gendered body

If defined by different sex organs, bounded and autonomous bodies come in genders, and, indeed, the earliest studies of gender took physical distinctions as an unproblematic given. An outgrowth of the women's movements of the 1960s and 1970s, gender studies began before the history of emotions took off. In its first phase, it simply took notice of the existence of women in history. Previously, historians had focused either on men and their activities or – as in the *Annales* school – on the social, economic, political, and geographical structures that underlay the sorts of things that mainly men did. The earliest studies to focus on women celebrated female artists, saints, queens, and Nobel prize winners – the "great woman" view of history. Or they considered the various roles – weavers, spinners, beer brewers, factory workers – that even nameless women had played in the past. These studies challenged the prevailing narrow definitions of both politics and power.[18]

Meanwhile, psychologists, too, were breaking away from their fixation on the male subject by looking at females as well. In the 1970s, the American Psychological Association set up a division on the Psychology of Women. Around the same time, Stephanie Shields, a pioneer in the field, wrote about "the psychology of women as it existed prior to its incorporation into psychoanalytic theory." This psychology, as Shields pointed out, was derived from a Darwinian model. It emphasized "the biological foundations of temperament," particularly "the maternal instinct," which it treated as "innate."[19] Shields did not, however, critique the research done after 1960 and up to her own time. Had she done so, she would have observed that of 139 articles dealing with women and emotion published between 1960 and 1975, as many as 125 (i.e. 89 percent) dealt with the emotion of depression. Moreover, such studies overwhelmingly took up "female" issues, namely matters associated with reproduction. Abortion engendered anxiety and depression; gynecological operations led to depression, anxiety, and loss of libido; pre-menopause brought depression, sorrow, bitterness, and apathy; and so on.[20]

These were "essentialist" studies that understood "female," and therefore "male," as fixed categories. Nor did historians writing in the 1970s directly question that assumption. Nevertheless, they were interested in exploring more than reproductive or other woes, and they were open to the possibility that "female" emotional lives in the past differed from those of today. Thus, when Carroll Smith-Rosenberg wrote about female relationships in nineteenth-century America, she interpreted the women's passionately affectionate letters and diaries to one another not as "abnormal" or "homosexual," but rather as part and parcel of a society that welcomed and valued same-sex love. The women whom she studied wed men, had children, and lived apart from one another. Yet their mutual love continued unabated. "My darling how I long for the time when I shall see you," wrote one woman to a dear friend, using language that today we associate with erotic love. Smith-Rosenberg suggested that amorous feelings between women served an important social function, ratifying the "rigid gender-role differentiation within the family and within society as a whole." She noted that the "emotional segregation of women and men" threw women together daily, often hourly. Women helped, comforted, and kept company with one another. Such closeness could have resulted in resentment, in unwelcome feelings of dependency or exploitation. Love, by contrast, made this sociability welcome – indeed, longed for. Similarly, but looking at Victorian England, Sharon Marcus found evidence of women happily enjoying close friendships, erotic bonds, and domestic lives with other women.[21]

Same-sex friendship was (and still is) a lively topic in the history of emotions, generally linked to the issue of homosexuality. When John Boswell found rituals that bound men together in what he called "obviously the same-sex equivalent of a medieval heterosexual marriage ceremony," he denied that these ceremonies were proof of homosexuality. Rather, he thought that the distinction between "heterosexual acts and relationships and homosexual acts and relationships was largely unknown to the societies in which the unions first took place." C. Stephen Jaeger argued that in the Middle Ages, love among men could be expressed with the most erotic language and yet have nothing to do with sex – and everything to do with ennobling virtue. Extending Boswell's argument was Alan Bray's history of same-sex friendships, tracing their entanglement with kinship throughout the long history of Western Christianity. Downgrading the importance of the nuclear family – mother, father, children – Bray documented "other kinds of kinship formed (as marriage is) by ritual and promise."[22]

Such an argument, without quite saying so, made the family a socially constructed rather than a natural institution. In the 1980s, the idea that gender itself was socially constructed became fashionable – with David Greenberg's *The Construction of Homosexuality*, Joan Scott's article on "Gender as a Category of Analysis," and Judith Butler's *Gender Trouble*. Nor was this idea the preserve of historians alone. Social psychologist Agneta Fischer debunked the "stereotypical view of female emotionality." In an article published in 2000, Stephanie Shields noted that "emotion ... has come to be viewed as fundamentally a social process. ... In my own work, I examine how emotion values and language are central to the concepts of femininity and masculinity and, as such, to the acquisition and practice of gender coded behavior." In an anthology put together by Penelope Gouk and Helen Hills in 2005, the editors asked, "whose body is under discussion in relation to emotions, their regulation and their control?" Their answer was the white, elite male body. Like Nicole Eustace, they spoke of the important role emotions had in creating and sustaining social distinctions. "Lower social classes, women and non-white peoples are, for a variety of reasons, [seen as] less able to subject their emotions to control." Assumptions about gendered emotions here upheld class and status.[23]

Historian Caroline Bynum rebelled against the sort of history that claimed a dualism at the core of the Western tradition, one that "despised the body" and "identified the body with nature and the female," pointing out that there were several conflicting traditions within the West, many of which did not accord with the stereotype. Christine Battersby offered the example of Enlightenment philosopher David Hume (d.1776): rather than separate reason from emotion, associating the former with men and the latter with women, Hume made certain passions utterly essential to the "reasonable" man.[24]

Indeed, new work on masculinity directly contradicts the modern stereotypes. Gerd Althoff called attention to the public tears of the bishop of Hildesheim, and Piroska Nagy found that for much of the Western Middle Ages, crying was understood as a virtuous act of moral purification, often considered a gift of God. Ruth Mazo Karras showed how the chivalric model included weeping knights. Even in the seventeenth century, when new, more Stoic notions of self-control prevailed, some versions of Galenic medical theory argued on behalf of tears as a healthful "purgative," and some elite circles cultivated them as a sign of refinement. But on the whole, as Bernard Capp shows, in seventeenth-century England (at least) "male tears represented an embarrassing loss of self-control." In the eighteenth century, however, the culture of sensibility made high-pitched emotions once again take center stage, with "the man of feeling" the key player – at least until women, too, began taking bows. A century later, during World War I, it seemed that a more emotional version of masculinity might be in the offing yet again, as some soldiers did not hesitate to express their feelings. But in the interwar period, as authoritarian ideologies took hold, the ideal of the emotional male petered out.[25]

When the dichotomy – rational men vs emotional women – was paramount, how did it function? A collection of articles edited by Susan Broomhall sees "the structuring of emotions into specific emotional states, and the imposition of gender ideologies, as works of power." Is the "structuring of emotions" always linked to the imposition of gender ideologies? The appositional commas in Broomhall's sentence suggest that it is. If so, Broomhall was making a connection that sociologists had been keeping separate. Indeed, sociologists Douglas Schrock and Brian Knop, wishing to overcome this separation, noted in 2014 that "although more work now addresses *both* gender and emotion, since 2000 it still accounts for only 3 percent of published articles on gender or emotion." Calling gender "a form of inequality," they took up three ways in which it was created and sustained: through socialization, intimate relations, and organizations. Inequality began with socialization early in childhood, when young people learned to use and expect emotions that reinforced male or female identities. Emotions like shame were used to steer boys away from trying on dresses. Emotions like anger were attributed to boys, fear to girls. These were "gendered feeling rules," and they were as significant in socialization as pink bedrooms for girls, blue for boys. In intimate relations – among family members – women were seen as the chief emotional negotiators: they ended up doing most of the "emotion work." In organizations, the separation of women and men into different kinds of work was buttressed by various gendered emotional assumptions. Finally, race and class complicated all these matters.[26]

By now, there are many historical studies of the socialization of children, both male and female, and some of them focus on emotions. In the hands of Susan Broomhall and her colleagues, emotions not only help construct gender, but also provide a way for hegemonic groups to assert authority. For example, one of Broomhall's authors, Stephanie Tarbin, found that both boys and girls in early modern England were expected to fear parental and other authority figures. But the fear was somewhat mitigated for boys, so as not to stifle their "spirit," whereas girls were to be entirely subdued. She found court records suggesting that girls, more often than boys, were subjected to fearful experiences, such as forced marriages and sexual assaults. However, another author in the same collection, Annemarieke Willemsen, found that late medieval and early modern schools in the Netherlands and neighboring regions educated both boys and girls. While boys generally went on to higher education, children of both sexes went to the elementary schools. There, although separated into different classrooms, both boys and girls followed nearly identical routines and, when misbehaving, submitted to similar punishments. The curricula for girls "overlapped with that of the boys in the usual subjects." The main difference was that girls also learned needlework and bookkeeping and were taught " 'womanly' virtues and behavior." Thus, no global generalization is possible.[27]

On intimate relations, numerous historians have taken up the challenge posed by Laurence Stone's depiction of the early modern family as loveless, even "unfriendly." According to Stone, noble and gentry families were organized to transmit property to their eldest son. But it is not clear that this involved *gendered* emotions. At the lower end of the social scale, children of both sexes "were neglected, brutally treated, and even killed; adults treated each other with suspicion and hostility." Historians have worked hard to refute Stone and to reveal affection within the early modern household, and a few have looked at gendered emotions as well. Emlyn Eisenach's study of Veronese families in the period, for example, suggests that in some cases, fathers and daughters had strong bonds based on affection, while in others "the notion of affection between spouses came to greater prominence."[28]

Schrock and Knop's research agenda moved from intimate relations to "organizations," in other words, to institutions apart from the family. These certainly shaped gender roles historically. There were male and female Franciscans, but the men wandered the streets of the cities, preaching and begging for their sustenance while the women were confined behind the walls of convents and were subject to a different set of rules. Were their emotions expected to differ as well? Did they in fact differ? Piroska Nagy and Damien Boquet are in the forefront of studying these sorts of questions. When speaking of "the conquest of mystical emotions," they argue that a kind of emotionality often associated with pious women – one that was public, loud, and expressive – in fact was adopted and practiced by men as well. Women wept constantly, ate nothing but the consecrated host, and went into ecstasies in church. The recluse Clare of Rimini hired two soldiers to whip her, in imitation of Christ's flagellation. Yet these emotional sensibilities and behaviors were not "marginal, nor uniquely the affair of women." They became widespread alongside the new emphasis of the Church on Christ's incarnation – on his human body. We see such sensibilities, argue Boquet and Nagy, among the flagellants (both male and female), in the mortifications – and the constant joy – practiced and felt by Saint Francis, and in the affective asceticism of men like Henry Suso, who cut the initials of Christ into his chest, right over his heart. Nevertheless, the roles of the men were different and so, to some degree, were the emotions. Men were the ones who wrote up the lives of the women, both offering them as models and controlling how those lives were to be interpreted.[29]

Yet that control was not total, for gender is sometimes, as today, a vehicle for self-discovery. Transgender, multigender, and agender people assert new identities and with them create new kinds of communities that respond to power – i.e. to the hegemonic norm – by defying and (if possible) escaping it. They explode the categories "male" and "female" with which historians of gender have hitherto been occupied. While historians have called gender a sort of performance and thus freed it from the biological body, they have nevertheless tended to work with two genders, however sexually oriented. Now they need to consider the possibility of other genders or no gender at all. Already psychologists are asking how non-female/non-male emotional lives have been (and are continuing to be) constructed, and they are considering the specific emotions involved in identifying as agender. For example, Douglas Schrock and his colleagues have explored the emotions expressed and longed for in present-day transgender support groups. Stephanie Budge and her colleagues have looked at the positive emotion themes found among transgender men (people who were born with female genitalia but identify themselves as male), including amazement, pride, and happiness. They conclude that positive interpersonal interactions encourage positive emotions, implicitly suggesting that the construction of gender needs emotional affirmation from therapists and others.[30]

Historically, gender transformations and identities have taken different forms, a fact that many historians have recognized. Caroline Bynum's pioneering article, "Jesus as Mother," pointed the way for much subsequent research. She noted the widespread twelfth-century imagery of Jesus and God as a woman and explored the significance of the new "emphasis on breasts and nurturing, the womb, conception, and union as incorporation." Men like Saint Bernard called themselves mothers: "As a mother loves her only son, so I loved you," he wrote to abbot Baldwin of Rieti. While Bynum did not explicitly say that Bernard took on an ambiguous gender identity when he wrote this (she was writing before the idea was current), her research implied conclusions along those lines. More recently, Kathryn Ringrose has claimed that eunuchs at the imperial court meant that "Byzantine society was not wedded to a rigid bipolar gender structure." Eunuchs had considerable prestige during the eighth to twelfth centuries, but both before and after that (when they were largely despised) they were categorized as a "third sex." This was not quite the same as a third gender, but rather signified an unnatural being – sometimes considered defective, at other times viewed as akin to angels.[31]

Rather little of this research has taken emotions into account, but Megan McLaughlin does so in her discussion of metaphors of the Church during the reform period of the eleventh and twelfth century. At that time, the gendering of the Church as a woman (a natural outgrowth of traditional views and of the grammatical gender of the Latin word for church, *ecclesia*) took on exceptional emotional resonance. "She" (i.e. the Church) was a vulnerable woman, variously old and wrinkled or young and beautiful, but in either case dependent on clerical men to protect and help her. She was also their "mother," and clerics expected her to love and care for them while they in turn owed her love and gratitude. But since these roles reflected those of "social reality" at large, clerical emotions were inflected by those of flesh and blood sons, who were largely independent of their mothers. This meant that in both familial and religious life "the bond between mother and child could generate anguish as well as honor."[32]

The "practiced" body

While gender research only gradually accepted that genders might be socially as well as biologically constructed, the study of the practices of the body took culture into account from the start. Drawing on the performative view of emotions, it stressed the role of the *physical body* itself in that performance. Already in 1989, French cultural theorist Michel Feher pointed out – in the introduction to a compendium of essays on the history of the body – that emotions are "immanent in the ceremonies that produce them." Treating the "love" expressed by troubadours for their ladies as a translation from "inside" (feeling) to "outside" (gesture), he asserted "not that the transports of love are artificial; but they do not exist outside a certain setting, that is, a stylization of movements and poses."[33]

Taking up this point systematically, Monique Scheer has more recently argued – drawing on Bourdieu's practice theory – that emotions are above all *practices of the body*. Putting together "doing" and "saying," Scheer stresses the bodily acts involved in every emotion. The importance of this theoretical move is clear when it is compared to Reddy's emotives. For Reddy, as we have seen, emotions are "activations of thought material," and emotives are speech acts that have "an exploratory and a self-altering effect on the activated thought material of emotion." Therefore, Reddy's emphasis is on thought material. Scheer's emphasis, by contrast, is on movement and utterance, which employs tongue, mouth, and muscles and impinges on the bodies of the self and others. Indeed, emotions involve "perceiving sounds, smells, and spaces." They are not newly born each time we feel something, but rather are entwined with habits and memories that are, in turn, bound up with our bodily movements and senses. Every emotion "must include the body and its functions ... as a locus for innate and learned capacities deeply shaped by habitual practices." Naturally, the historian of emotions is limited by her source materials, but that means searching even harder to find not only written texts (which will always remain of paramount importance) but also "images, literature, musical notation, film, or household items." Words alone, in Scheer's view, are at best desiccated fossils of lived emotion. She wants historians to be "thinking harder about what people are *doing* and to working out the specific situatedness of these doings."[34]

An example of Scheer's method is her discussion of the religious practices of the Methodists who followed Christoph Gottlob Müller (d.1858), a German butcher and vintner. Becoming a Methodist while spending some time in England, he adopted their bodily practices – their constant singing, sitting, standing, and kneeling. These, along with their emotionally intense sermons, implied a particularly strong emotional commitment. When Müller returned to Germany, he introduced this style of worship to people who already had some of this "bodily knowledge" as it had been shaped by their local Pietism. But the Methodists had forms of pious practices beyond Pietism – at church meetings penitents wept, sighed, groaned, fell to the floor – and Müller worked to make these movements habitual (see Plate 5). The body not only expressed feelings but also created and reinforced them.[35]

Scheer's "multimedia" approach was further developed by her colleagues at the Max Planck Institute, Margrit Pernau and Imke Rajamani. They looked, for example, at the emotional message of "love in the rain" – the final scene of the Bollywood film *Veer Zaara* – which

> ends dramatically, the protagonists meeting again after spending most of their life separated, each sacrificing their future and present for the other. They finally come together in an encounter, set as a song sequence, in which the musical gestures and composition of images signify the intensity of their emotions. But the protagonists do not speak a single word that might indicate how to interpret the depicted feelings.

How can the researcher know what those feelings are? "The scene would be lost for a history of concepts that focuses only on language." But listen to the melancholy music, and the words of the Hindi song, look at the close-ups of the lovers' happy, tearful faces, and above all consider the symbolic meaning of the rain in which the reunion takes place: "the monsoon [is] a season of erotic love, and torrential rain

[is] a sign of longing and fulfillment." In Pernau and Raja-mani's telling, the viewer's very body feels the emotions in the movie through "a multisensory experience." This idea draws on current film theory, which postulates two interacting bodies – that of the film and that of the spectator – and sometimes goes still further, to stress the "haptic" nature of vision whereby, in the words of Jo Labanyi, "viewers abandon themselves corporeally to the flow of images on screen."[36]

Not all discussions of emotional practice draw upon Scheer. Laughter, for example, has been of interest to historians, even before the turn to bodies. For psychologists, laughter is a cross-cultural, even cross-species universal. Darwin said it was the particular expression of joy and illustrated it with the photographs in Plate 1. Freud related laughter to unconscious impulses. Ekman, following Darwin, considered a large smile the signifier of happiness. Thus, it was natural for historians of emotion to talk about laughter as well, though it figured rather little in the initial approaches surveyed in Chapter 2. Reddy did not discuss it at all; Rosenwein took it up only as an "emotion marker" – a bodily sign of feeling – and Althoff's emphasis was far more on signals of grief and anger than on emotions related to laughter.

Classicists, however, had always been interested in the gestures of rhetoric, which were, in part, designed to elicit the audience's emotions. Thus, it is not surprising that one of the first major studies of laughter's history was written by a professor of Greek, Stephen Halliwell, who wanted to understand laughter "within [a] wider investigation of [ancient Greek] cultural forms and values." While admitting that laughter is "a deeply instinctive gesture," Halliwell understood it nevertheless to "generate expressive protocols and habits with complex social ramifications." Those protocols and habits were the subject of his book, and they were complex indeed, for the Greek world appreciated many different sorts of laughter, connecting them to, on the one hand, immorality (Plato), and on the other, immortality (the laughter of the gods). In between were the many and various uses of laughter in friendship and enmity, praise and derision, shame and honor, and numerous other social situations. Nor was all laughter bodily: then as now, you could "laugh at someone" without literally laughing, and when poets said that the weather "smiled," laughter became a metaphor for mildness and charm. But not always, for the many significances of laughter changed over time. Indeed, more recently Mary Beard has taken up "laughter as a shifting and adaptable cultural form" in ancient Rome.[37]

Medievalists found similar diversity and change in the Middle Ages. Already in 1999, Jacques Le Goff demonstrated in the compass of thirteen pages the wildly varied uses of and attitudes toward laughter, a point made once again in a monumental collection of essays edited by Albrecht Classen. Although ancient Greek had words that differentiated smiles from laughter, Latin long had only one word, *risus*, to mean both. Only in the twelfth century did a new word appear for the smile: *subrisus*, literally a "suppressed laugh" or a "little laugh."

In the eighteenth century, the smile came into its own. Colin Jones speaks of a "smile revolution," and connects it to the French Revolution. It was part of the new "sentimentalism" that played so important a role in Reddy's understanding of the emotional underpinnings of the rebellion against the ancien régime. The new Parisian smile was also fueled by innovative forms of dental care that sought to preserve, not pull, teeth; and it was galvanized by changing notions of beauty, personality, and identity. Yet, the smile's new status in the eighteenth century did not extend to laughter, which had far more ambiguous significance. "The manner of laughing, its intensity, as well as the causes of this human behavior were the essential criteria by which the superior classes were distinguished from the society of common people." Indeed, while today the open-mouth smile is considered the marker of happiness and a social signal of cheerful friendliness, Jones makes clear – in a conclusion to the first of a three-volume collection on the history of emotions – that this is a very recent "habitual practice," a sort of hybrid between the gross humor of the bawdy Rabelaisian laugh and the demure upturned lips of Leonardo's "La Gioconda."[38]

The porous, merged body

"Laugh, and the world laughs with you" wrote Ella Wheeler Wilcox.[39] Emotions are contagious. They pour into the world

– into things and the interstices between things. The newest
approaches to emotions take us out of the bounded body and
towards a different conception according to which the body
merges with what is outside of it. Historians of emotions
are increasingly interested in the ways in which "bounded"
bodies are in fact unbound. They study this phenomenon in
four ways: as affects permeate the world; as bodies define and
are defined by space; as the body imprints and is imprinted
by matter; and finally, as the body incorporates both space
and matter in what we may call "mental space."

The affective body

For Silvan Tomkins (see Chapter 1), affect was "the primary
innate biological motivating mechanism." Today, affect theorists stress the ways in which the affective, energized body
intersects with other bodies, things, and spaces. Affect may
begin in the physiological body, but it ends up pouring into
the world.

While affect theory is fairly marginal to the interests of
many psychologists, it has been widely embraced by scholars
in literature, cultural studies, communications, and philosophy.
We need to explore its main tenets because of its increasing
interest to historians. Indeed, the International Society for
Cultural History named the "affective turn" the overall topic
of its 2017 annual meeting. While the theory has many facets,
perhaps the most important is how it reconsiders the body.

The affective body is "contagious," open and unbounded.
It is constantly sharing itself with the world of things, people,
sounds, and smells around it and absorbing them in turn.
It is so involved in the world that the boundaries between
us and everything else are erased. Yes, we have a biological
body; but it is nothing without its surroundings, which shape
it, just as it shapes the environment in turn. Subjectivity is
largely a social construction: we are who we are because of
our experiences and habits; those will change as we continue
to have relationships with other, equally porous, bodies, and
so we will change as well. According to Sara Ahmed, "bodies
take the shape of the very contact they have with objects and
others." Bruce Smith explains this point with the analogy of

"the visual puzzle presented by the vase that can also be read as the profiles of two faces": the body is known only by its surroundings, and the surroundings have meaning and take shape only with our bodies. Indeed, anything we touch has that same double character, for what we touch defines the thing, just as the thing suggests what we are touching. Smith sees even texts taking on our "profile," as they in turn shape us. Think of how we are "changed" by reading a poem into which we, like it or not, read ourselves.[40]

At the start of their introduction to modern affect theory, editors Gregory Seigworth and Melissa Gregg define the term: "affect ... is the name we give to those ... vital forces insisting beyond emotions ... Affect is persistent proof of a body's never less than ongoing immersion in and among the world's obstinacies and rhythms." Unpacking this, we may say that for these two theorists, affect "insists" in a way that emotions do not. They are more intense than emotions: they "stun." That is why psychologists Stein, Hernandez, and Trabasso can claim that "a pause almost always occurs between the affective and emotional responses." Indeed, affects may inhibit "access to any thinking and planning" – that is, they may inhibit emotion itself. Philosopher and affect theorist Brian Massumi emphasizes affect's forcefulness:

> Intensity is embodied in purely autonomic reactions most directly manifested in the skin. [It is] a nonconscious, never-to-conscious autonomic remainder. It is outside expectation and adaptation. ... It is narratively de-localized, spreading over the generalized body surface, like a lateral backwash from the function-meaning interloops traveling the vertical path between head and heart.

According to this view, while "function-meaning loops" – such as emotions and the words that we use to describe them – make a beeline from heart to head, affect is their directionless, delocalized "backwash."[41]

Seigworth and Gregg's definition continues with "affect's always immanent capacity for extending further still: both into and out of the interstices of the inorganic and non-living." Here they stress the ways in which affect enters spaces and places that are not necessarily alive but are nevertheless enlivened by our own subjectivities. When we walk into a room we feel its atmosphere, communicated by smells, sounds, perhaps touches and tastes as well as sights. We feel its tenor and we contribute to that tenor in turn. The "inorganic and non-living" themselves become affective bodies.

Affect theory works best for the contemporary world, where numerous kinds of primary sources are available, but it may also be applied to materials from the more distant past. An example is Bruce Smith's treatment of Shakespeare's Sonnet 29: "When, in disgrace with fortune and men's eyes." Smith wanted to recover "the felt experience" of this poem: the experience of Shakespeare while he was writing it, certainly; the experience of Shakespeare's contemporaries while they read the poem; and, finally (because, given the nature of affect, we cannot separate ourselves from what we are reading), our own experience while we make sense of it.

To mimic what writing the sonnet felt like to Shakespeare, as well as to appreciate it fully as an affective body composed of far more than words, Smith asks his readers to copy the poem out by hand. This will make it "theirs" in a way that mere reading will not do. Smith insists that a book is a physical object with which we interact. It is "something I hold in my hand, using my fingers and thumb as an easel. ... The book remains an object 'out there' even as I *in*-corporate 'in here' the words printed on the page." The very words of the page are acts – speech acts. Scheer and the performative school already said that, but Smith pushes further. For him, the words are "bodies-in-space-in-time." He means that the words on the page may be understood to take up space and unfold over time. He makes this point clear by consulting an American Sign Language (ASL) specialist. Signed words are bodily gestures in space that follow one another in real time. When Smith asked the signer to perform Sonnet 29, he discovered that in ASL the pronouns of the poem took on new and unexpected meanings: they invited the viewer to merge the "I" of the poet with the "you" of the audience. The gestures for lines like "[I] beweep," and "[I] look upon myself," implicates the viewer with the subject. Indeed, "[I] look upon myself," likens the "I" of the poet to the viewer peering from the outside.

Smith's overall point is that affect theory makes us see, contemplate, and feel the poem beyond words, to the place before words were ever formed. He argues that affect theory *avant la lettre* existed in Shakespeare's own day, so that the reader then also felt the pre-verbal poem. His proof is the *Chirologia: or the Natural Language of the Hand* by Shakespeare's near contemporary John Bulwer (d.1656), who theorized that gestures preceded words. Bulwer saw gesture as taking thoughts "from the forestalled tongue," that is, before the tongue could utter anything at all. This allowed Smith to read the text of Sonnet 29 as a series of meaningful pre-verbal gestures in space, communicating affect through movement. The actual words of the poem did not limit its meaning to the reader/interpreter. And the words that mattered most were unexpected: the pronouns (me, he, she) and the prepositions (to, from, with) that created relationships between people.[42]

The performative approach to emotions is already quite close to affect theory. Considering the Declaration of Independence as a performative means treating it as both the product of a performance (men deliberating beforehand, then signing it) and a "performer" (impressing us with its size, its fonts, its parchment, its language). The affective historian must go a bit further. She sees the words within the Declaration as invitations to think about relationships. She considers that the words are only the final step from "thought without speech" to "verbal thought." That is, words leave much unsaid. They are like the gestures in Bulwer's *Chirologia*. Every word – but this is especially easy to see with the pronouns – is like one of Reddy's emotives, implying many meanings even as it expresses just one. The first sentence of the Declaration moves from "one people" to "them" and their connections with "another," and then implicitly turns to "you" – those hearing or reading the document. You know (or should know, the Declaration implies) that the Laws of Nature and of Nature's God entitle "them," "the other," *and* "you" to "separate and equal station." The Declaration doesn't say in words, "you and we and even they are in agreement about this," but implicitly it assumes just that. In this largely grammatical analysis of a text, the focus is, even so, on a "body." But it is a body of many parts, for it includes the text itself, its writer, its signatories, and its readers.

Relatively few historians have adopted the affective turn unreservedly. In this they mirror many psychologists, some of whom have introduced the term "cogmotion" to express "the interactive and inseparable nature of cognition and emotion." Historians critique affect theory for various reasons. Ruth Leys argues that Massumi and other affect theorists misuse the scientific data that they cite. Some historians are uncomfortable with a theory that asks them to include their own emotions in their research. Still others object to downgrading the importance of words in favor of pre-verbal reactions.[43]

Affect theorists are aware of the irony of a stance that undermines words while using them – indeed, while using them abundantly, luxuriantly, and poetically. Affect practitioners appreciate this irony, finding it fitting for their slippery topic. Seigworth and Gregg make clear that they rejoice in the indeterminateness of affect: "There is no single, generalizable theory of affect: not yet, and (thankfully) there never will be. ... Such a state of affairs might ... go some distance toward explaining why first encounters with theories of affect might feel like a momentary (sometimes more permanent) methodological and conceptual free fall."[44]

The body in – and as – space

The body moves in spaces and places, giving them meaning; at the same time, spaces and places assume cultural and individual meanings that affect people in turn. This is a social constructionist view, and it first came of age in the 1960s, closely associated with the work of philosopher Henri Lefebvre. However, Lefebvre was not a historian, and his ideas about how people, feelings, and spaces interacted were general and global.[45]

More recently, historian Margrit Pernau, for one, has gone beyond Lefebvre, denying that there is "a universal body, affected by space and materiality in any simple and unequivocal way." Looking at spaces in the planned city of Old Delhi, in India, she noted that "the same narrow lanes, which created a feeling of security for elder men, might feel claustrophobic for their sons." Later generations might feel still differently – or, indeed, feel nothing at all, as the original significance of some places might "lose their readability, even before they are transformed into different material spaces."[46] Pernau's insistence on "readability," was an answer to the phenomenologists and affect theorists who, as we have seen above, consider the preverbal experience to be primal, even today.

Affectual geographers (those who adopt affect theory) argue that people are affected by spaces in ways that are entirely unconscious and must remain forever unexpressed and inexpressible. Spaces themselves – where the transpersonal experience of affect may be seen most clearly – have agency, causing affective changes. After all, space is defined by things and people: the space of a house is determined by its walls, windows, and objects; the space of a street by buildings, people, animals, cars, and so on. Space causes affective changes because bodies of every sort – human, non-human, transparent, dense – have affective capacity. In the words of geographer Ben Anderson, affect is "a transpersonal *capacity* which a body has to be affected (through an affection) and to affect (as the result of modifications)." Affect is ineluctable; the body *has* to be affected and to affect in turn. But, Anderson warns, "there is not, first, an 'event' and then, second, an affective 'effect' of such an 'event.'" Affect is always happening.[47]

Certainly, some geographers prefer to talk about emotions expressible through language. Steve Pile's useful overview of both kinds of geographies – emotional and affectual – points out that emotional "geographers have described a wide range of emotions in various contexts, including: ambivalence, anger, anxiety, awe, betrayal" and the list goes on, ending with worry. These are understood as "ways of knowing, being and doing." Even affectual geographers, despite their insistence on wordlessness, have talked about "anger, boredom, comfort and discomfort, despair..." and their list, too, goes on. After all, they must use words to say what they think.[48]

Both sorts of geographers have concentrated on reactions to surroundings, but Joyce Davidson and Christine Milligan emphasize the body itself as a space filled with emotions and with emotions themselves having spatial dimensions, as in "the 'heights' of joy and the 'depths' of despair." We infuse spaces with our feelings (viewing them "with rose-tinted glasses") just as spaces move us. Their discussion pushes outward, from the body and emotions at home to institutions (schools, factories, prisons), to cities and rural areas, and eventually to the nation and beyond.[49]

Historians are interested in this work, but they also want to stress the historical dimensions of space. In 2012, Benno Gammerl published a collection of essays designed "to open up new vistas on the history of emotions." The contributors considered how emotions were connected to spaces within certain "socio-cultural contexts." As readers may imagine by now, not all the essays used the same definitions of emotion.[50]

For example, Andreas Reckwitz used the terms affect and emotion interchangeably, criticizing sociologists who saw a dualism "between rationality and irrationality." Such dualism turned emotions and affects into "individual traits not suitable for social generalisation and/or as natural and biological structures or drives." Seeking to overcome these binaries, Reckwitz proposed (again much like Scheer and Pernau) to focus on "social practices" to provide "an integrated heuristic framework for an analysis of affectivity and spatiality." Indeed, the integration was easy, for "*every* social practice" involves both emotion and artefact-space structuration; and insofar as emotions are "directed at artefacts/objects" they are structured in turn "by the spaces these artefacts/objects form." Since practices are always social and cultural, they are subject to historical change. But why should they change at all? Why not remain practiced and re-practiced for time out of mind? Reckwitz took Peter Stearns's ideas into account here: as advice manuals changed their discourse, they led to changes in practice. To this, Reckwitz added the effect of "changing assemblages of artefacts in space." Technological changes are easiest to see; Reckwitz cited by way of example the new feelings that were evoked when trains were first invented; their closed cars hurtling through the countryside provoked emotions never before experienced.[51]

Train cars, city squares, streets in Old Delhi are all particular constructions. But some historians writing for Gammerl's collection thought of space functionally: households, courtrooms, circuses. Mark Seymour called these functional spaces "emotional arenas." He noted that "historical actors, while they may appear to belong to one particular emotional community, are likely to shift their allegiances, values, and modes of expression according to the expectations they associate with a given spatial arena." (Rosenwein, whose "emotional communities" were invoked here, would agree. But she would put it differently; she would say that arenas help us see the full dimensions – both the flexibility and the limitations – of an emotional community's expressive capacity.) Seymour's essay considered a criminal trial that took place in Rome, in a church that had been repurposed as a court of justice by the newly minted late nineteenth-century Kingdom of Italy. Seymour argued that this space was a place "in which to perform, witness, and adjudicate the emotions of a new nation." Describing the sober and restrained demeanor of the lawyers and prosecutors, Seymour contrasted it with the flamboyant and seductive emotional displays of the defendant, Pietro Cardinali, a circus acrobat from Calabria accused of murder. Neither the legal community nor the performer changed their emotional behavior within the courtroom: the space did not here function to determine emotional styles. Rather, the emotional styles themselves were put on trial there. Indeed, the "trial" took place as much in the press as in the courtroom: one journalist, for example, described Cardinali as displaying "a permanent cynical smile [and] an affected self-confidence," eliciting in the writer "an invincible repugnance." When the grand chief prosecutor asked for the death penalty, "this was an emotional high point in the trial, and a journalist reported that ... the audience murmured with lively sensation, 'as if a shiver made its way through the auditorium.'" Yet, Seymour did not conclude with the triumph of one emotional community (that of the lawyers and state officials) over another (that of provincial circus performers). Rather, he argued that the courtroom became a place for the new nation to reconcile the styles of its peripheries (like Calabria) with the center (Rome).[52]

In this view of space as "functional," collections edited by Broomhall are once again prominent. *Emotions in the Household* takes up the various kinds of emotions that were forged (or obstructed) in households. Unlike courtrooms, which must be of a certain size and contain architectural features necessary for a trial, households need not have any physical or spatial features apart from size; they simply must be large enough for more than one person. Tracy Adams' essay in this collection explored very wealthy households in early modern France. Some of the most prestigious of these took in foster-girls from lesser noble families, who paid considerable sums to have their daughters raised by members of the elite. The girls joined households of "at least 100 members, spread throughout different divisions – the bedchamber, the kitchen and the stables." Taking two texts as revealing the emotionology of such fosterage – one by Christine de Pisan (d.*c*.1431), the other by Anne of France (d.1522) – Adams argued that the emotional standards of these noble households stressed "peacemaking" and amiability. "The relationship between girls and their mistresses, and among the girls themselves, was meant to be one of mutual love." Adams understood this to be an ideal, but she argued that it might have been real as well. If so, she saw it as providing solace for girls who were, in effect, pawns in the social ambitions of their families. Another essay in the same collection, this by Ivan Jablonka, looked at a similar phenomenon – fosterage – in humble peasant households. Wards of the state, the foster boys and girls were not legally or biologically family members. But their letters – as well as official reports – revealed that the fostering relationship "was affective, spiritual and social," resembling the bond between parents and children. Did the "space" really have much to do with the emotions? It doesn't seem so: Jablonka found that the affective relationships between wards and their fictive parents were quite different from the relations between masters and apprentices or servants, even though all lived under the same roof.[53]

This brings us back to Stephanie Tarbin's study, where the household was an arena for emotions far from affectionate love. She stressed the ways in which early modern English households privileged fear, awe, and dread. This does not prove Pernau's point about the variable meanings of space across generations or for different groups. Rather, it is evidence that historians use the term "space" in incommensurate ways. Pernau used it as Lefebvre had, as a precise place: this street, that park, my house. But for Broomhall and her contributors, space was much less specific. The household is a conceptual space, and the concept is in the minds of historians. In the words of Broomhall, "We adopt a broad definition of the concept of 'spaces for feeling' here: they are understood as communities formed by a shared identity or goal (or aspiration towards these), practised through a specific set of emotional expressions, acts or performances, and exercised in a particular space or site. These spaces could be physical or conceptual."[54]

The body and matter

From the seminal works of Daniel Miller to those of Arjun Appadurai, Alfred Gell, and many others, material culture has largely been the preserve of ethnographers, anthropologists, and sociologists. It is now among the most "recently discovered" topics in the history of emotions. Things, materiality, and the object/subject dyad arrived on the radar screens of historians of emotion around 2002, when a two-day roundtable discussion organized by Gerhard Jaritz was held in Krems, Austria, its proceedings published the year after. At the end of that meeting, Barbara Rosenwein called the pairing of emotions and material culture "a site under construction," an interesting metaphor given that many of the papers were about the destruction, theft, or plundering of property.[55] As we shall see, the site is still only partially built up.

A bit before the Krems roundtable, archaeologist Sarah Tarlow asked how researchers might get at emotional *subjects* when only *objects* are available. How could archaeologists theorize emotions? Tarlow ruled out "naïve or positional empathy," arguing that we could not assume "that past emotions are knowable because we can imaginatively experience them." Nevertheless, after rejecting the universalist view that people of the past felt precisely as we do, she conceded that "our shared experience of being human provides us with a basis for the interpretation of, for example, sensory perception." Indeed, she was willing to go so far as to say that our ancestors had "the capacity and proclivity for experiencing emotion, though not necessarily the experience of specific emotions." But how could the archaeologist go beyond the bland assumption that people always had emotions? Tarlow was writing before affect theory had taken off; even so, she anticipated something like it: "It is ... important for us to theorize the materiality of emotional practices. What are the relationships between spaces, architectures, artefacts, and emotions? How do things become emotionally meaningful?"[56]

Archaeologist Chris Gosden sought to answer Tarlow's questions via aesthetics. Accepting the idea that emotions are a sort of judgment and therefore imply a kind of intelligence, Gosden argued that judgments of beauty – or, more generally, "the values we attach to the formal qualities of objects" – were emotional as well as rational. Gosden chose the case of a carving held to be a sort of human being by the Te Arawa people of New Zealand, arguing that its return to its ancestral house in 1997, after a 120-year absence, was a moment of high drama and feeling. Drawing on Reddy's notion of emotives and Butler's of performatives, Gosden argued that the "multi-sensorial nature of our engagement with the physical world quickly takes on the complexity of an emotional experience." Indeed, it *is* an emotional experience, which, though impossible to put fully into words, is enacted through our bodies.[57]

By 2010 affect theory had arrived in archaeology departments. Oliver Harris and Tim Sørensen drew on it "to understand how people and things bring their worlds into being." By way of example, they proposed to analyze the emotions and affects that were involved in building, using, and transforming a large henge enclosure at Mount Pleasant in Dorset, England, built *c.*2500 BCE. Drawing on Gell's notion that works of art affect people immediately, regardless of the purposes of their creators, Harris and Sørensen developed and employed a "new analytical vocabulary" of four terms: atmosphere, attunement, affective field, and emotions. In the concrete instance of the henge, Harris and Sørensen postulated that the 176 wooden posts of the original inner enclosure, far smaller than the eventual construction project, constrained certain sorts of bodily movements and mental perceptions. That was its *atmosphere*. But as that atmosphere changed (as, for example, when the wood decayed), people's *attunement* changed. Consequently, their *affective field* – their "relational connection" with the place and one another – changed as well. And as this new affective field demanded new behaviors, those "differing kinds of bodily movement ... would have helped to elicit *emotions*."

After exploring the possible affective meanings of the entire site, Harris and Sørensen concluded that "people felt required to return [to the henge] because of the potent histories revealed in the site's architecture and materiality, a potency

engendered through the textures generated by the people's
emotional engagements and feelings of community." Now,
while no doubt the henge was built, used, and reused by one
or more communities, speaking of "feelings of community"
makes something of a leap. But it is the only specific feeling
the authors allowed themselves to mention, for all the rest
was fairly generic: potency would be true of any site with
cultural meaning. As Sarah Tarlow pointed out in a subsequent
review of the literature on emotions and archaeology, Harris
and Sørensen were among those archaeologists who limited
themselves to showing "how a more loosely specified emotional
power shaped particular moments, places, and relationships."
She spoke of those who had "engaged more closely with a
particular emotion," and called on her colleagues "to explore
the social, cultural, and, in the broadest sense of the word,
historical aspects of emotion, which I argue must focus on
its variability."[58] In short, simply saying that people "were
moved" by a site is not enough.

Tarlow is an archaeologist making common cause with
historians. Yet, compared with archaeology, history was tardy
in putting together emotions and material culture; the subtle
interplay of the two did not gain currency until around 2010.
Following Tarlow's own lead in an article on graveyards and
gravestones (where writing intersects with materiality), historians of emotions turned first to cemeteries. As Tarlow noted,
"gravestones lie between archaeology and text; their proper
study demands consideration of their materiality as well as
the inscriptions on their surface." She found that, by the nineteenth century, gravestones were explicitly emotional, evoking
"loss, love, and grief." But even long before the nineteenth
century, as Rosenwein showed for the sixth and seventh centuries, a wide variety of sentiments were embedded in funerary
inscriptions. Still earlier, as classicist Angelos Chaniotis pointed
out, people in the Hellenistic world carved words – not just
on tombstones, but on all sorts of durable materials and in
every sort of public space – to express envy, hatred, love,
despair, lamentation, consolation, and many other emotions.
But neither Rosenwein nor Chaniotis considered the stone's
agency itself, nor anything pertaining to what medievalist
Jeffrey Cohen called the "enduring vivacity" of stone, describing its agency in poetic language: "Stone does not carry story

passively forward, tractable surface for inscription. The lithic is tangled in narrative: prod as well as hindrance, ally as well as foe, a provocative and complicit agency."[59]

While Cohen's book deliberately avoided "the totalized products of human shaping, such as statuary," art historian Elina Gertsman explored the emotional significance of medieval anthropomorphic sculpture. Putting texts and images together, she challenged the idea that smiles signified happiness. In fact, she argued, smiles were ambiguous. The Gothic sculptural theme of the Wise and Foolish Virgins (a parable in Matthew 25:1–13) aptly illustrated her point. The biblical story of the Virgins makes clear that if smiles express happiness, then the Wise Virgins will smile (for they will go to the Bridegroom's feast, a metaphor for Heaven), and the Foolish Virgins will weep (for they are locked out and will end up in Hell). The smiles on the statues of the Virgins at Magdeburg Cathedral (carved *c*.1250) are as predicted: the Wise ones smile blissfully; the Foolish Virgins, by contrast, wipe their tearful eyes and frown. But at Strasbourg Cathedral, the same story is given a twist (see Plate 6). Carved only thirty years after the Virgins at Magdeburg, the Strasbourg Virgins, whether Wise or Foolish, do not smile. There is one exception, however. A figure alongside the Foolish Virgins is young, handsome, and smiling, but snakes and toads crawl up his back. He is Satan, and the Foolish Virgin nearest to him, as Gertsman points out, "grins radiantly." Here her smile is not a sign of happiness but of stupidity and sinfulness.[60]

The Virgins are fairly easy to "read" emotionally because they represent people, and their significance is indicated by a biblical text. But what if the historian is confronted with something apparently emotionless as, for example, a piece of cloth? Even here, historians find it hard to abandon the cocoon of textuality. In a collection entitled *Everyday Objects*, Catherine Richardson discussed the emotional meaning of two special hats purchased in 1560s England. Depositions in ecclesiastical court records, in suits involving breaking the promise of marriage, show that the hats were, at the very least, tokens "of affection and of coercion," for the woman's acceptance of those hats implied betrothal. On the other hand, in the very same collection Lena Cowen Orlin argued against the "Victorian legacy" that makes us "sentimentalise objects." In her view, even "tokens" and "remembrances" in wills "were generally represented as carriers of economic worth, and little more." By this approach, Shakespeare's gift to his wife of his "second-best bed," may have had "symbolic value [e.g. as a sign of respect] and financial value, but no recoverable sentimental value." Wills are clearly slippery texts, their lapidary provisions provoking a myriad of interpretations. When Shakespeare willed his "second-best bed" to his wife, was this an expression of husbandly indifference; a sign of special love; or simply a way to ensure she would have something to sleep on?[61]

No matter how slippery texts may be, when John Styles studied the tokens left with babies abandoned in the mid eighteenth century at the London Foundling Hospital along with letters or short phrases inscribed on cloth, he praised the combination of words and things as the "great strength of the Foundling archive as a historical source." Like Tarlow, Styles assumed that "shared human experience" linked past and present emotions. He observed that "the presence of these objects in the archive arises from one of the most profound experiences of separation and loss known to human beings – the rupture of the foundational emotional bond between mother and baby." Given this premise, why did Styles question the "authenticity" of that very bond? Do these objects – asked Styles – "tell us how poor mothers felt about giving up their babies, or do they tell us how poor women thought a wealthy institution would expect them to express emotions about separation and loss?" He drew on the general cultural significance of some of the objects to tackle the problem. Colored silk ribbons – predominant among the Foundling tokens – were well-known "symbols of love, especially in circumstances of separation and loss." So, too, were hearts, "an established symbol of love in the eighteenth century," generally left in the form of fabric tokens (see Plate 7). In the end, what Styles found essential for those mothers, far beyond their sporadic recourse to words, was the "language of ribbons and hearts" that was "accessible to all."[62]

Like Styles, whose work falls into the category of "public history," social anthropologist and museum curator Tove Engelhardt Mathiassen found cultural meaning in ribbons. Her article appeared in an issue of the journal *Textile: Cloth and Culture* devoted to evaluating the connections between "fabric and feeling." Each essay considered a different sort of textile important in Northwest Europe, *c.*1620–1910. Making three crucial assumptions – that the meaning of the textiles changed over time; that mainly women, not men, were affectively connected to fabrics; and that each material itself had its own peculiar emotional potential depending on its texture, look, and smell – they included in their purview the emotions of the women who wrote the articles. Thus, Mathiassen confessed that "a specific set of clothes made me emotional" while working on an exhibit of early modern Danish baptismal garments. Above all, the tiny size of one cap forcibly brought home to her the vulnerability of the newborn child and its need for protection. But did the child's parents feel the same way? Without textual sources, "knowledge of emotions connected to these specific clothes seemed to stop at a dead end." Like Styles, Mathiassen found an indirect route, drawing on the beliefs and values embedded in Danish culture at the time. Knowing about the high infant mortality rate, and following her own sensibility about the child's vulnerability, she looked at many elements – some woven directly into the christening garments – that together suggested protective strategies and therefore parental concern and love. For example, starting *c.*1700 most such garments were red, or had red decorations such as ribbons. As was true in England around the same time, the ribbons were a symbol of love, while the color red in Danish folklore was thought to ward off evil. Red was connected to Christian religious thought as well: it was "a powerful color used as a symbol of love, passion, and blood." Employing this same approach with metal elements (threads, charms, or pennies sewn into a cap or gown or hidden in a pocket) and rituals of reuse (as with a mother's wedding dress turned into a christening garment), Mathiassen concluded that the emotions inhering in material objects could be interpreted even if they could not be read.[63]

Such emotion is "inherent" in material objects because of the meanings assigned by people. Can objects have their own emotional agency? Absolutely. In a much-cited article, Sara Ahmed spoke of "happy objects." The editors of *Emotional Textiles* talked about fabric's "emotive properties."

Plate 1 Smiling faces in Darwin's *The Expression of the Emotions in Man and Animals* (1872).

Three smiling girls cascade down the left side of this plate, matched by three apparently smiling images of one man. But the man is not really smiling: his picture was taken as part of an experiment conducted by G.-B. Duchenne de Boulogne, who applied electrical stimuli to his patient's paralyzed facial muscles. For Duchenne and Darwin, the artificial nature of his smiles made the man's expression of emotion all the more "objective."

(Below) **Plate 2** American Airlines stewardess, mid to late 1960s.

A jaunty smile lights up the face of this stewardess as she serves a meal. She is the model of the successful airline employee who, as sociologist Arlie Hochschild would put it, has learned through unrelenting "emotional labor" to feel the cheerfulness that she displays.

(Right) **Plate 3** *The anger of Saul, the tears of David* (Winchester Bible, *c*.1180). These scenes in an English medieval manuscript illustrate Gerd Althoff's point. In the top tier (left-hand panel), King Saul stands ramrod straight, showing no emotion as he wages war against the Philistines. In the middle tier, however, he is bent out of shape, signaling his anger and displeasure with David, whom he envies. Below is the moment just before the murder of Absalom, King David's estranged son. The final scene shows David in mourning: raising the edge of his mantle to his eyes, he performs his grief with a gesture already well-known in classical antiquity.

(Below) **Plate 4** The Declaration of Independence (July 4, 1776).

This engraving makes the Declaration's physical features very clear. Starting with the bold "In Congress," it recalls the look of documents issued by English kings, in effect proclaiming the official status of the fledgling United States. Its many grievances are separated by spaces marked by thick black strokes, suggesting the outrage of the scribe and the signers, and performing its indignation for all subsequent viewers.

(Right) **Plate 5** A Methodist camp meeting (*c.*1829).

A preacher gestures to the sky; men and (even more obviously) women raise their hands, groan, shout, kneel, and fall down in a faint. Dogs sniff and mingle; men and women gossip; a bugler pipes his horn. The tents in the background reveal that the participants in this early nineteenth-century Methodist camp will remain for several days. They are "practicing" their emotions.

(*Above*) **Plate 6** The Foolish Virgins at Strasbourg (c.1280).
A jolly young man holds up an alluring apple, attracting the young woman at his side. She is one of the Foolish Virgins about whom Matthew 25:1-3 spoke, and she is more foolish than even Matthew recounted, for she is flirting with the Devil himself. As the two grin heedlessly, they signal not happiness but moral depravation.

(*Left*) **Plate 7** Textile red heart token (18th century).
A beaded red heart had no need for words to explain its significance when it was pinned to the clothing of a baby left at the London Foundling Hospital. Across all social classes the heart was understood as the vital principle of life, the centre of true feelings, the place of love. Its red color was reminiscent of blood. This particular heart token has been creatively personified.

Plate 8 *BioShock* screenshot (2007).

In this screenshot of *BioShock*'s final in-game cinematic (or non-interactive sequence), one of the Little Sisters – her face showing certain filmic conventions – offers Jack the key to Rapture. In this happy ending, Jack refuses the key, while the voiceover of Dr. Tenenbaum, one of the characters, is full of grateful emotion.

Jeffrey Cohen declared that "stone contains energy and radi-
ated agency." He recalled that a tear of Anglo-Saxon Bishop
Erkenwald was said to have effectively baptized a cadaver,
releasing its soul to heaven: "Erkenwald's affective and material response binds the living and the dead in story."[64]

Thus far, all the approaches we have discussed began with
material objects and then tried to tease out their emotional
(or, sometimes, non-emotional) significance. But there is
another approach: to start with an emotion and see how it
is expressed materially. Already at Krems, Daniel Smail began
with enmity and then argued that in late medieval Marseille
people pursued their enmities through the distraint of goods.
He considered, for example, a squire who "seized two silver
cups *auctoritate propria* [on his own authority] from the shop
of Bertran de Velans, described in the [legal] record as 'his
enemy.' " In *Love Objects*, the authors began with love and
then explored its material manifestations. While most of the
contributors worked with contemporary objects, Elizabeth
Howie documented how nineteenth-century male–male romantic relationships were expressed in photographs of rapturous
embraces and mutual adoration, and Ann Wilson (in a paper
more about religious emotions than about love) sketched the
historical context (Ireland in 1920) in which some Catholic
devotional images were said to bleed, a phenomenon that at
one and the same time enhanced the power of the Church
and threatened to undermine it.[65]

Finally, some authors begin with emotional practices that
by their very nature involve objects. Cultural critic Rey Chow
explored the many "libidinal ramifications" of collecting. On
the one hand, disdain for the human "love-of-things" may
provoke bonfires, as happened during the Chinese Cultural
Revolution in the 1960s. On the other hand, it may turn into
a love affair: the collector's social relationships and sense of
self-worth focus on things; they are objects of devotion; without
them, the collector no longer wishes to live. But Daniel Smail
had a very different interpretation to offer for the related
practice of hoarding. He coupled it with consumerism and
the epigenetic environment in which it flourishes, arguing
that hoarding might well be connected with certain lesions
and perhaps genetic conditions that were potentially available
in every age of human existence. However, it is expressed

behaviorally only in the environment of consumerism, which stimulates the serotonin system.[66]

Mental space

Serotonin brings us back to the physiological brain. But today the brain is also considered the site of memory and imagination, creating worlds with their own spaces and objects. Philosopher Martha Nussbaum has argued that books, music, plays, playacting, and other arts offer essential spaces in which to feel – not because they provide venues so much as because they stimulate mental scenarios. Spectators of a Greek tragedy, for example, imaginatively apply to themselves the emotions expressed by characters in the play. In effect, the drama "invites [them] to have emotions of various types toward the possibilities of their own lives."[67] Art and play offer space for emotional experimentation.

Does this imaginative space have a historical dimension? In the American Victorian period, women's sentimental literature offered more than its surface meaning, argues Marianne Noble. A poem written in 1827 by Maria Brooks invoked women's "beauty meek," but its masochistic imagery in fact created "a dark fantasy of erotic love," allowing its readership to circumvent "prohibitions on both female embodiment and female artistry." Sentimental literature created some possibilities for "self-exploration," making "available a language of passion, desire, and anger."[68]

Ute Frevert's team at the Max Planck Institute has written an entire book – *Learning How to Feel* – on the space of emotional imagination in modern children's books. The authors point out that children's books as a genre did not exist prior to the end of the eighteenth century. Gradually, they took hold thereafter, reflecting the new conviction that children did indeed have emotions, and, since they did, it was necessary to understand and above all shape those feelings. The subtitle of *Learning How to Feel – Children's Literature and Emotional Socialization, 1870–1970* – reveals the team's overall conclusion: that children's books worked to socialize rather than to encourage emotional imagination. The authors looked at advice literature alongside books for children, arguing that the two mirrored one another. If, as Frevert's team argued, children learn emotions by imitating and practicing them, then children's books offered models that children could admire, detest, and in general "try on." But those roles were hardly limitless. Treating in separate chapters a number of especially "social" emotions – trust, shame, compassion – and considering mainly the books popular in Germany, Scandinavia, and England, the authors showed that, on the whole, children's books offered rather restricted moral lessons that young readers were supposed to take to heart. Certain historical trends were quite clear: at first, children's books emphasized God's will or adult authority. Later, they granted greater standing to the child's peer group and asserted the moral equality of adults and children. Claims of European racial and Christian religious superiority slowly faded but never entirely died out. Gender roles equalized, and, in the most recent children's books, room was made for same-sex love and parenting. Thus, emotional space expanded over time, but beware: "these manifold opportunities and growing possibilities also became a new kind of duty ... [opening] the gates for a never-ending process of self-improvement and optimization." In other words, greater freedom for self-realization brought with it an endless search for identity.[69]

In their emphasis on the didactic teaching implicit in children's books, Frevert's group to some degree was swimming against the current. As the members of her team themselves recognized, it is one thing to see what the writers of children's books *want* children to learn, but quite another to know what imaginative fantasies such books offer to any individual child. Jan Plamper considered the possibilities for the young Russian readers of the adventures of the brave little boy Kesha: they could "share Kesha's experience of fear and bravery" and even go beyond that, "trying on" other emotions evoked by the story. Scholars less circumspect go so far as to imagine readers rebelling against the emotions propounded by books. Sarah Bilston contrasted the teachings of Victorian advice books with the "transgressions" implicit in Victorian girls' literature. Following literary theorists who say that readers themselves produce the meaning of a text, Bilston argued that the Victorian insistence on reading "reductively" for pious moral meanings was undone by actual reading patterns. Her examples – Charlotte Brontë's *Jane Eyre* and George Eliot's *Mill on the Floss* – were barely mentioned in Frevert's collection. But for Bilston these were good instances of the ways in which children's books upended Victorian values. She pointed out that in *Jane Eyre* the eponymous heroine read a book on geography and let her imagination wander. Jane was especially drawn to the illustrations "because of their mysterious open-endedness, the suggestive lacunae apparently left for her to fill." Even so, Jane's reading (and fantasizing) was by no means entirely free; for example, although she hated the Psalms, she knew them – and other pious texts – very well. Similarly, the heroine of George Eliot's *Mill on the Floss* made up stories to go with the books she read and, above all, their illustrations, getting thrills even from "an image of a drowning witch in Defoe's text [*The History of the Devil*] ('It's a dreadful picture isn't it? But I can't help looking at it.')." Thus, as Bilston interpreted it, "scenes of literary consumption in *Jane Eyre* and *The Mill on the Floss* illustrate and facilitate the production of unorthodox young heroines."[70]

Likewise, Rachel Ablow used Jane Eyre as the model of the Victorian reader: Jane, who is reading Bewick's *History of British Birds*, "is less absorbed in the text before her than actively inventing her own narratives on the basis of the materials and psychic space it provides." Jane herself reports, "I was then happy: happy at least in my way." Nicholas Dames, in a contribution to Ablow's book, went further, arguing that it was not just novels that offered space for affective imagination, but also Victorian critics of fiction. When they reviewed novels, they encouraged the reader to experience them through their very reviews by including prolonged excerpts that worked as "affective prompts." In another essay, Kate Flint observed that the Victorian novel served as a comfortable emotional escape hatch for readers far from home, insulating them from the unwelcome feelings that their immediate surroundings offered them.[71]

In a book on nineteenth-century upbringing practices in India, Ruby Lal considered the restricted lives of women and girls, who were expected to toil all day and obey male wishes and rules. Yet, these women and girls found spaces for imaginative playfulness and daydreams, undoing normative expectations, and feeling emotions that were officially unavailable to them. Working with texts invariably written by men, [ ] nevertheless uncovered traces of oral traditions that revealed spaces where girls and young women could express and feel forbidden desires, yearnings, and contradictory emotions.[72]

Dreams provide another mental space in which we feel strange, wayward, and powerful emotions. In *Dreams and History*, scholars in various disciplines considered the traditions of dream interpretation leading to, varying from, and partaking in Freud's landmark *Interpretation of Dreams*. Some contributors suggested the possibility of producing "a cultural history of dream contents and of repression." Others pointed toward a history of "the private perceptions and deep conflicts of men and women in other epochs." Exploring women's dreams in early modern England, historian Patricia Crawford considered how often they revealed deep emotional attachment to God. "I am as pent milk in the breast, ready to be poured forth & dilated into Thee," wrote Anne Bathurst in 1693. It was no accident that Bathurst used maternal imagery here, for women thought deeply – and dreamt – about emotional relationships with members of their family. Thus, Lady Wentworth wrote to her son, "Thees thre nights I have been much happyer then in the days, for I have dreamt I have been with you." Crawford argued that such dreams, recounted and repeated by appreciative audiences, afforded women a voice and an authority that they otherwise lacked.[73]

Crawford did not see these women's dreams as carving out mental space but rather as having a real-world function. Similarly, Robert Kagan's book on the dreams of Lucrecia, a young Spanish woman living during the sixteenth-century Inquisition, focused on their political meaning – as, indeed, did Lucrecia and her contemporaries. In both England and Spain, dreaming women found that a prophetic or visionary voice gave them power. Men, too, dreamt of politics. Or, at least, medievalist Paul Dutton chose to look at the "fewer than thirty dreams and visions from the ninth century that contain political matter." Those dreams – dreamt mainly by monks and clerics – told contemporaries what was wrong with the Carolingian political order and the terrible punishments that were in store, particularly for sinful kings.

Whether these dreamers had emotions was not Dutton's affair. But already in 1981, Peter Dinzelbacher's study of medieval visionary literature included a short section on "Emotional Reactions." Considering the impact of dream spaces, Dinzelbacher found that early visions vividly described scenes of threat or joy, whereas later visions were bland in both backdrop and feeling. But not all later visions were insipid. Jean-Claude Schmitt has analyzed the visions of Richalm von Schöntal, a thirteenth-century Cistercian monk, who saw demons and angels everywhere around him and everyone else. These beings populated the monastery, but he alone could see and hear them. Richalm used a highly developed emotional vocabulary, ranging from anger, weariness, and sadness to utter joy to describe his reactions. His whole body was involved, feeling pain, laughing and blushing. But he thought of these experiences in moral and spiritual terms: the demons were bad, the angels were good, and his emotions (or what we would call his emotions) were virtuous or sinful. Here mental, spiritual, physical, and physiological spaces were utterly merged.[74]

*

Whether bounded or open, gesturing or in pain, in households, courtrooms, churches or on city streets, whether asleep or awake, the body pulls the strings of much of the recent scholarship on the history of emotions. What will happen to the field in the future? How will it develop? What impact will it have on other fields and disciplines? In the next chapter, we take up some of the many opportunities and challenges that lie ahead.

4
Futures

> "There is absolutely no reason to believe that in about thirteen years
> we won't have hardware capable of replicating my brain. Yes, certain
> things still feel particularly human – creativity, flashes of inspiration
> from nowhere, the ability to feel happy and sad at the same time –
> but computers will have their own desires and goal systems."
>
> Sam Altman, President of Y Combinator, quoted
> in Tad Friend, "Adding A Zero," *New Yorker*
> (October 10, 2016)

While we do not yet have "hardware capable of replicating"
our brains, we have both hardware and software ready to
influence and express our brains, minds, and hearts. What
role does the history of emotions have in the modern world?
What role should it have in the future? The present chapter is
our quest to peer into the future and imagine new paths. We
divide it into two main parts. In the first, we explore issues
specifically linked to the field of history and its practitioners. In
the second, we ask how the insights of the history of emotions
are being – and ought to be – diffused to the wider public.

The walls of the academy

Emotion is a topic for everyone and on which all have something important to say. But the academic world sets up bar-
riers to such communication. The old grouping of "arts and

sciences," which put the humanities (the arts) and the sciences together, is increasingly obsolescent. History departments and history books themselves are divided by periods – ancient, medieval, and so on – that have become separate areas of research, interest, and expertise. The history of emotions has the potential – and the need – to tear down these walls.

Joining the history of emotions to the science of emotions

In a recent issue of the interdisciplinary journal *Emotion Review*, historian Peter Stearns criticized his fellow scholars. Historians of emotions used to read sociologists, anthropologists, psychologists, and philosophers and addressed those groups in turn. But as the history of emotions burgeoned, the field turned inward, speaking only to other historians or, even more narrowly, to other historians within a particular field of specialization (United States history, the Early Modern period, and so on). Insofar as it still exists today, "interdisciplinarity" has come to mean interacting with scholars in the humanities – in music, art, and literature. The gap between the sciences and history is now wide, and, concludes Stearns, "I do worry that this may involve some real loss to all parties."

With regard to shame, for instance, Stearns thought that a historical approach ought to be of keen interest to psychologists and sociologists. Nevertheless, historians had not been invited to the table. Why? In part, it was their own fault: they themselves, Stearns charged, had not addressed the history of shame since the 1980s, avoiding the question of "what happened after shame began to decline in the United States." But it was also the fault of psychologists and sociologists, the experts who are in the position to guide us and our child-rearing practices: they see no need for history. Had the historians done their work, and had the others listened, Stearns believed, all of us would understand why shame today – internalized and turned into self-deprecation – generates anger and violence, whereas in the past (and today in some non-Western cultures) it served to reinforce social cooperation. If today's psychological experts read historians, they might even modify their advice. They would learn from the past how, at one point in their history, Americans reintegrated those whom they shamed, and they might use this knowledge as a therapeutic tool. If they read histories, they would become more sensitive to the persistence of shame as an emotional undercurrent in at least some groups within our society. Furthermore, since the 1960s, Stearns argued, shame had made a "comeback" with the rise of social media.[1]

Scientists do not always neglect history.[2] But they do so often enough. Their voices have come to dominate over other disciplines, with (since the 2000s) neuroscientists ascendant in the field. Cornelius's textbook on the science of emotions (see Chapter 1), published in 1996, had an appendix on neuro-psychology. By contrast, the same topic is treated in a full chapter in Paula Niedenthal and François Ric's textbook, published in 2017. This helps explain the strategy of another article in *Emotion Review*. Calling for interdisciplinarity, psychologist Ad Vingerhoets and psychiatrist Lauren Bylsma outlined an ambitious research plan to understand crying. They wanted to investigate whether the causes of crying changed in the course of a lifetime; how gender differences functioned in instances of weeping; and the uses of shedding tears both for the person who was crying and for those around him or her. They called for "multidisciplinary collaboration," listing the disciplines that should work together on their project: "psychology, psychiatry, evolutionary biology, neurobiology, neuroscience, anthropology, and ethology." While ethology is the science of animal behavior, history is – strictly speaking – the science of human behavior over centuries. Yet, it apparently did not occur to Vingerhoets and Bylsma to include historians.

In fact, historians have studied weeping (see Chapter 3). While Vingerhoets and Bylsma knew about many positive and negative "antecedents of crying" in the modern world, they did not consider that, within the history of the West, attitudes oscillated between admiring tears and repudiating them. As Nagy showed, the ability to cry – before the Cross in a church, for example – was at one time a marker of sanctity, cutting across class and gender boundaries. The decline of this notion began within the intellectual elites of the thirteenth century. Two centuries later, during the Reformation, tears were associated mainly with sorrow for sin, not signs of blessedness. At that point, they rarely brought comfort to those who shed them. In their article, Vingerhoets and Bylsma posed a paradox: that while people think that "crying generally helps them to feel better," in fact "crying ... does not always result in mood improvement." For historians, this is not much of a paradox: even today, tears hang on to – and continue to echo the meanings of – half-forgotten but still potent traditions concerning tears.[3]

One of the reasons that Stearns gave for the historical profession's isolation from other disciplines was the fault of historians of emotions themselves. They had come to see their "contributions in terms of staple historical topics – the nature of the Renaissance or the experience of specific wars – rather than as explicit additions to the general field of emotion research."[4] Some historians of emotion do indeed still think of themselves as working in their own period of specialization. But in an interview with William Reddy, Barbara Rosenwein, and Peter Stearns, Jan Plamper asked "In which direction should the future history of emotions move?" Stearns wanted more "interdisciplinary bridges," while Reddy answered that "the history of emotions is a way of doing political, social, and cultural history, not something to be added to existing fields." Rosenwein said something similar in an article published in the same year: "Just as issues of gender are now fully integrated into intellectual, political, and social history, so the study of emotions should not (in the end) form a separate strand of history but rather inform every historical inquiry."[5]

The ideal future would in fact involve *both* the integration of the history of emotions into other kinds of histories *and* its incorporation into scientific inquiries. We can certainly see how the interests of historians and scientists might converge beyond the rare moments offered by venues like the *Emotion Review*. The recent interest in the body, explored in Chapter 3, has affinities with the focus of some scientists on the multiple neural pathways between touch and feelings. We say "your tears touched me" and "you hurt my feelings," both of which may well be more than metaphors. Neuroscientist David Linden has written recently of the emotional aspects of the sensitive envelope that contains us – our skin. He is well aware that "context is key in sensory experience." The same touch "feels" different when it is applied variously by a lover, a doctor, or a mother. "Our perception of a sensory stimulus is crucially dependent upon our expectations, as they have been formed by our life experience up to that moment." Historians can add to "life experience" factors such as standards of feeling, communities, genders, spaces, and regimes in the past. Nevertheless, at this point scientists are less interested in contexts than they are in discovering the separate neural circuits that differentiate our many sensory and affective experiences.

Not all such scientific inquiries are equivalent to those that identify different areas of the brain with specific emotions. In other words, some researchers work well with theories that stress interactions within the neural networks of the brain and life experiences. Cyriel Pennartz speaks of an associative network "underlying mental processes such as memory, attention, discrimination and evaluation of sensory inputs, and voluntary control over behavior." A new book by psychological constructionist Lisa Feldman Barrett forcefully argues against what she calls the "classical view" of emotions – the view that (whether in the body or mind) emotions are universal "triggered reactions." They do not come in discrete units like "anger," or "shame." Sam Altman knew this (recall the epigraph that opens this chapter) when he spoke of human beings as having "the ability to feel happy and sad at the same time." Emotions are constructed from the person's real life experiences and perceptions of the world and the body. Scientists like Barrett and historians of emotions have much in common. The major difference is that historians know that those real-life experiences depend as much on the past as on the present.[6]

Overcoming periodization

As Stearns pointed out, historians themselves carve up their own field into discrete units. Historians must decide to "major in" one or another period; they present themselves as classicists or medievalists or modernists when they apply for jobs, and they read the books and articles that are pertinent to their area of specialization. Historians of emotion cannot quite follow form in this regard. They have to keep up in their "field," but they also must read at least some scientists, anthropologists, archaeologists, and literary theorists. They must read one another, even outside of their specialty. This is partly because historians of emotion must still hone their methods, approaches, and assumptions. But there is another good reason: emotions, perhaps more clearly than other historical subjects, are palimpsests. Consider again the weeping that posed such a paradox to Vingerhoets and Bylsma: people *think* they are comforted by crying, but in fact often are not. The history of weeping reveals that the authors were witnessing traces of earlier patterns of feeling, behavior, and thought, but now uneasily transferred into a modern setting. A historian might (in our view, should) say that modern feelings about weeping contain within them the whole history of tears. Indeed, generalizing, a historian of emotion might say that there is not a "new and modern" way of feeling as opposed to the "old" feelings of the past, but rather that today's emotions are amalgams of past ways of feeling adapted to the present.

If this is so, it blurs the distinctions between "periods" of history. Western civilization courses, for example, are built around three major eras: ancient, medieval, modern. But periods, like emotions, are not preordained. We think that the history of emotions may – indeed *must* – help to tear down the walls.

Of course, there are good reasons for historians to talk about periods. They are obliged to deal with both stasis and change, and to manage this duality they "periodize" – that is, they decide when one age ends and another begins. The traditional view is that grand shifts justify new period labels. The late Jacques Le Goff, a medievalist who chafed against the notion of a period "in the middle," nevertheless argued for "a long Middle Ages" that extended all the way to the mid eighteenth century. There he found justification – primarily in industrialization – for calling the next period, *c.*1750 to the present, the "modern" era. As Le Goff put it, in the 1700s it became "possible to leave one period behind and leap forward to the next." Despite his revision of the names and lengths of his historical periods, this view is nevertheless very traditional in conceiving of periodization as a series of leaps and landings or entrances and exits.[7]

But this is not the only possibility. Relevant to the history of emotions is Reinhart Koselleck's argument for upsetting categories of periodization. According to Koselleck, political and social concepts contain within them past, present, and even future. When, for example, we consider the notion of "equality" in the Declaration of Independence, we need not only to understand the meaning of the word to Jefferson and to his contemporaries, but also to see alive within that meaning a whole Western tradition. Moreover, the concept of equality in the Declaration contains the future as well, since when *we* read the Declaration, we impose on it our own understanding, one that extends to our expectations of what is to come.

Koselleck's way of looking at history asks that we modify our ideas about periodization. If all periods use concepts composed of "multiple overlapping layers," then there is no one moment when everything changes. Koselleck was not thinking of emotions, but because emotions are palimpsests, they are very much like his "concepts." Additionally, Reddy's "emotives" are very similar to Koselleck's "concepts" in that each emotive, like a tiny bomb, explodes with multiple meanings that are (all at the same time) potentially in play. While Reddy does not dwell on the historical dimensions of emotives, his discussion of romantic love suggests that its very history, including its novel use by the troubadours, continues to resonate in our own day, despite "modernity" and "industrialization," and all the other things that normally set off the present from the past.

Rosenwein's notion of emotional communities adds another dimension to this idea. Many of the practices, habits, and values of an emotional community persist (sometimes fully, sometimes transformed, sometimes repurposed) over centuries. Stearns's recent article on shame makes this point: despite a general decline in both talking about and experiencing shame, "some groups were surely more susceptible to the shift in fashion around shame than others. ... [Recent historical work] would suggest that Evangelicals had more reason and capacity to retain a shame emphasis than many other groups. ... More broadly, emotions history does encourage subcultural tracking and explanation."[8] Here Stearns, like Rosenwein, stresses that at any given moment of time there are multiple emotional communities. Although they may be entirely isolated from one another, they often influence each other, whether through borrowing, repudiation, or (typically) both.

The history of emotions suggests that periods should not be conceived in terms of "leaving" or "leaping forward." "Traveling" is a better metaphor, as people move through gradually changing landscapes. They wear some of their traditional clothing and pack what they think they will need in their valises; but as they travel, they also shed some items and add others, responding to their altered circumstances and needs. Emotions, unlike clothing, cannot be purchased. But they can indeed be learned or borrowed and thus added. In short, historians of emotions are well poised to suggest some of the precise baggage taken, added, repurposed, and cast off over the long haul.

Diffusion within and beyond the academy

The history of emotions has implanted itself in the web and within institutional landscapes especially in France (with EMMA), England (with Queen Mary University of London), Australia (at the Center of Excellence of the University of Western Australia), and Germany (at the Max Planck Institute), even as it has many practitioners in the United States, Italy and elsewhere. It has also inspired several book series.[9] These are important indications of its success within the academy. Yet with success come problems and challenges. In one sense, EMMA itself was already a reaction to success: it is resolutely Francophone rather than Anglophone, while all the other institutions and blogs use English. This "Anglophone dominion" is in part a legacy of scientists, whose meetings and publications are nearly always in English.

However, outside of academic settings the impact of the history of emotions has been very slight. This is a pity. Thus, envisioning a future in which the historical layers of emotions will be drawn upon, alongside the findings of many other disciplines, we consider two influential products of today's culture – children's books and videogames – that may help us glimpse the promise of such a future.

The challenges of success

In 2007, the University of Western Australia's Center of Excellence won a $24.25 million government grant over the next seven years to study the history of emotions. Other comparable centers benefit similarly (though in lesser measure) from generous funding. What explains this outpouring of interest and money? And what are – or might be – the consequences?

The first question may be answered quickly. We (in the West) live in an age fascinated with emotions. In one week in April 2017, the *New York Times* had 37 articles that mentioned emotions, whereas it had, for example, four such articles during the same week in 1945. The United Nations sponsors a "Happiness Day"; in its annual Happiness Report for 2017, it declared that Norway "tops" the "global happiness rankings." Google's Ngram Viewer, which allows users to search word frequencies in sources printed between 1500 and 2008, shows that the use of the word "emotional" in English-language books more than doubled between 1920 and 2000. *Why* emotions have become a cultural obsession is another question, no doubt requiring an extended answer. However, the failure of the great theoretical constructs of the nineteenth century or of traditional religious outlooks to explain the human condition is probably the chief reason. Emotion has become a substitute explanation for what used to be considered governed by ineluctable social, political, or religious laws.[10]

The result of all the support is a flood of publications. When so much money is allocated to a field; when so many people are supported by that money; when institutions and individuals hope for continued funding; when publishers need books and journals need articles, then expectations are very high for new publications – and lots of them. While it is hard not to welcome all the new contributions to this growing field, it is also true that many are fragments that do not fit together terribly well. In *The Slow Professor*, Maggie Berg and Barbara K. Seeber suggest that these are not problems limited to the topic of emotions. Counseling a calmer publishing schedule and a smaller number of publications, their book has itself an emotional purpose: to make the academic life less anxious and pressured – both for teachers and students.[11]

The media

Beyond the classroom are all the other venues of culture and experience. Children – indeed, all of us – learn from books, newspapers, and magazines, radio and television programs, music, movies, videogames. Many of these media are now potent communicators of the *science* of emotions, both implicitly and explicitly. But their creators have not yet taken advantage of the new dimensions and conceptual tools offered by the history of emotions.

Many of today's children's books unabashedly draw on Ekman's paradigm. While they do not necessarily adhere to six or seven basic emotions (*The Way I Feel* has thirteen) they associate each emotion with a facial expression (and, often, a color). *On Monday When It Rained* closely echoes Ekman's original experiment in that it sets up scenarios and associates them with one correct emotion. For example: "On Monday when it rained my mother said I couldn't play outside. I wanted to ride my new red bike with the blue horn to my friend Maggie's house. I was..." [next page] "Disappointed" ... [next page] a photograph of the "disappointed" face of a child who in fact posed for all the emotions in the book. Ekman's theory also feeds into the current rage for emoticons, the ubiquitous circular "faces" that bestrew our social networks. Probably first developed in the 1960s, all are known as "smileys," though by now they stand in for a great variety of emotions, and not just the cheerful message of the original.[12]

Beyond Ekman, authors often draw on some version of cognitive theory. In Cornelia Maude Spelman's *When I Feel Scared*, a small bear lists all the things that scare it: "I feel scared when there's a big, loud noise," it says, while the picture shows the resultant action, as the little bear crouches down, holding its paws over its ears. Later, it finds solutions to its fear – in hugs from its mother; in talking things over; in learning that everyone is afraid sometimes. Fear management also involves avoiding the sources of fear, so the little bear thinks, "I shouldn't climb too high, play near cars, or go near fire." The book is part of a series, "The Way I Feel Books," that also takes up anger, worry, jealousy, and sadness (among other emotions), explaining to parents that "education about how to identify and handle our emotions (especially those that are unpleasant or frightening) is as important as other kinds of learning.[13]

Jamesian theory is represented by *Angry Octopus*, a do-it-yourself guide in which children are taught "how to use progressive muscle relaxation and breathing techniques to calm down, lower stress, and control anger." A social constructionist view is presented in Roger Hargreaves' *Mr. Happy*: the protagonist lives in Happyland, where everyone smiles and is happy. He meets Mr. Miserable, who has not been living in Happyland and wears a permanent frown. Discovering that Mr. Miserable would prefer to be happy, Mr. Happy brings him to his cottage "for quite some time. And during that time the most remarkable thing happened. Because he was living in Happyland, Mr. Miserable ever so slowly stopped being miserable, and started being happy."[14]

Charming as these books are, it must be observed that Ekman's faces, cognitive theory, Jamesian approaches, and even automatic social constructionism are blinkered and simplistic in ways that may be less helpful to children than their authors hope. We do not suggest that such authors read more history, but we do propose that they start to think more like historians in their willingness to accept ambiguities and multiple layers of feeling.[15]

We urge much the same for videogame makers. Right now, cognitive psychology and Ekman's faces dominate the field. We briefly begin with films, for they have supplied videogame designers with some of their most potent techniques for emotional expression and evocation. Yet, even films have not taken advantage of emotions history. At best, filmmakers consult historians when their films are set in the past. For example, in 1982 director Daniel Vigne asked Natalie Zemon Davis to collaborate with him on *Le Retour de Martin Guerre* (*The Return of Martin Guerre*), a movie about a sixteenth-century imposter who posed as the absent Martin Guerre, married his wife, took over his property, and fathered a child. Nevertheless, like all directors, Vigne had the priorities of a filmmaker, while Davis had those of a historian. After the film was released, Davis felt the need to write a book that would present the case more accurately. "Writing for actors rather than readers," she observed, "raised new questions about the motivations of people in the sixteenth century – about, say, whether they cared as much about truth as about property. ... At the same time, the film was departing from the historical record, and I found this troubling." This is hardly the first time that accuracy and creativity (not to mention box office attraction) have collided.[16]

In the last twenty years, film studies have sought to shed light on the emotional techniques of filmmaking. They have considered several aspects, including the effects of narrative itself; the use of close-ups to "read" (and sympathize with) the emotions on characters' faces; the ways in which music "cues" the emotions of the viewer; and the safe spaces that films and theaters provide for every sort of feeling. While filmmakers generally resort to their own emotional repertories and instincts, critics largely (if not exclusively) draw on cognitive views of emotion. Thus, in the words of Amy Coplan, "cognitive film theory has produced a rich literature on spectators' emotional responses to narrative fiction films, but almost all of it has focused on sophisticated emotional processes involving the imagination or cognitive evaluations." For her part, she proposed to add "more primitive emotional processes and reactions," namely, the notion of "emotional contagion" advanced by social psychologists like Elaine Hatfield. In the end, whether concerned with cognitivist mental assessment and action readiness, or with the idea that the emotions of the people around us are contagious, no film commentator has considered the lessons of the history of emotions.[17]

Contemporary videogames have much in common with films. Startling improvements in both technology and design have granted players unique cinematographic experiences. As early as 2004, Dave Morris observed that, in addition to their enhanced esthetic qualities, videogames were improving in content and "acquiring depth, beauty, and emotion." In large measure, these were the legacy of films, deriving especially from their focus on characters. As Guillaume de Fondaumière of videogame company Quantic Dream once declared, "Our work is like movies because movies to a certain extent depend very much on character and ultimately emotion." From the time

when game designers, reviewers, and commentators started
to think beyond the games' electronic and technological features to the "experience of playing," emotions became central.
How did videogame creators elicit emotions in players? How
did they involve players in the lives (and deaths) of their on-
screen characters? The narrative dimension of videogames and
the keen sense of agency given to players were the essential
tools. Indeed, as pointedly argued by Bernard Perron and Felix
Schröter, "it is when discourse of videogames and narrative
became more important that videogame emotions began to
be a pivotal topic in game studies and design research."[18]

That discourse began a while ago. Already in 2000, Steven
Poole wanted videogames "to try to expand their nuances of
emotional impact interactively." To do that, they needed "a
game system that is able to create an interesting and evocative
story even out of really dumb decisions by the player, a huge
and perhaps insurmountable challenge."[19] True enough, and the
challenge prompted colossal improvements in both videogame
narrative and gameplay. But did players' agency develop beyond
those "dumb decisions"? And did these advances enhance the
emotional experience of players?

Hypothetically, game developers and experts should be free
to draw upon many different emotions and emotion theories.
In reality, they have limited themselves to rather few. With
a background in psychology from Stanford, Nicole Lazzaro
– founder in 1992 of XEODesign, Inc. – described herself as
"the first person to use facial expressions to measure player
experiences." Much influenced by Ekman, Lazzaro's group
arrived at a practical model in 2004 – "The Four Keys to
Fun" – to help game developers craft emotions to enhance
gamers' experiences. "Pulled from the facial expression of
hundreds of players, this trend-setting research lays the foundation for gamification," proclaims her company's website.
Her research identified more than thirty emotions that mirrored an expanded list of "basic emotions" published a year
earlier in Ekman's *Emotions Revealed*. Lazzaro was writing in
2004, but even today Ekman tends to dominate the conceptual
frameworks in which videogame emotions are inscribed. At
least one juror of the Emotional Games Awards established
in 2016, Erik Geslin – a self-described specialist in "emotions
induction in video games and VR" – holds the FACS (Facial

Action Coding System) Coder Expert certification developed by the Paul Ekman Group.[20]

Other videogame consultants draw on "life itself," as David Freeman puts it. Exploiting his background in screenwriting, Freeman developed techniques – collectively termed Emotioneering, a neologism combining emotion and engineering – to create emotional games through evocative characters and narratives. Freeman's website, advertising his expertise to the people in the videogame industry, explains that when games are emotionally compelling, "they'll get better player 'buzz.'" He goes on to list further advantages: better press coverage, increased sales, and even a happier work force, for, as he claims, game developers will "pour more passion into their work." Emotioneering offers 300 techniques in 32 categories. Its "First-Person Deepening Techniques," for example, take up ways to involve the avatar – the player's character – in emotionally difficult choices. Its "Plot Deepening Techniques" prescribe methods to create emotionally powerful narratives.[21]

In *Video Games and the Mind*, Perron and Schröter criticize Freeman and other theorists of emotional game design because they "failed to theoretically ground their concept of emotion." They consider more recent game theory to be better grounded because it draws, as does film theory, on cognitivism. There is good reason for their optimism: videogame developers used to focus mainly on the emotions involved in the actions and interaction demanded by gameplay, leading them to think mainly about excitement and amusement. But developers wanted more, and this they found, inspired by films, in better, more compelling, and more emotionally involving stories. In the wake of that development, Perron and Schröter adapted for games the cognitivist approach of film theorists. In their words, cognitivism "offers the most comprehensive accounts of contested concepts like identification, empathy, or mood," and it "readily lends itself to theorizing emotions elicited by interactive works such as games." Furthermore, since games directly enlist bodies – a point extensively covered by Katherine Isbister in her recent book, *How Games Move Us* – Perron and Schröter argue that "the recent *body turn* in cognitive media studies makes this research even more fitting to describe the complex ways of engaging with videogames." At the very least, those ways involve arms, hands,

and wrists on keyboards, mice, and gamepads; or they use
the whole body in motion gaming. Altogether, Perron and
Schröter label "cognitive game studies" the collective endeavor
of the contributors to their book, with the great advantage
that it "doesn't isolate itself from other paradigms – like, for
example, cultural studies of games and play, philosophical
and phenomenological perspectives on players and playing,
or empirical studies of affect and emotion." It goes without
saying, however, that the history of emotions is not invited
to this court's banquet.[22]

If there is one game that entails all the issues of gameplay,
narrative, players' agency, empathy, moral assessments, and
emotional engagement, it is the highly successful *BioShock*,
developed by Irrational Games, published by 2K, and released
in 2007. The story of Jack and his vicissitudes in surviving
the dystopian underwater city of Rapture, *BioShock* requires
players to make a choice: to gain extra-human abilities by
"harvesting" the substance they need from the young girls
(the Little Sisters) who carry it, or to spare the Little Sisters
the brutal harvest that causes their death. Eventually, this
choice – reiterated throughout the videogame – leads to three
different endings: in the closing cut-scene, the voice of one
of the characters expresses approval if the player has spared
all the Little Sisters; outrage if the player has harvested them
all; and sorrow if the player has spared a few and harvested
others. The prize for sparing all the Little Sisters is "a family,"
as the young girls, now grown up, educated, and married, put
their hands in that of Jack (the player's avatar), apparently on
his deathbed. In her study of child characters in videogames,
Susanne Eichner argues that their function "is less to allow for
processes of identification than to enable empathic reactions
that range from sympathy, care, worry, and feelings of loss to
parental concern for the characters, which, in turn, are likely
to influence the game's overall emotional atmosphere." With
regard to the Little Sisters, Eichner notes how the player is
"confronted with a set of filmic conventions, such as facial
close-ups on widened eyes, frightened faces, or the repeated
image of the lonely girls huddling together and crying," a set
of formulas meant to convey the logic of childhood innocence
(see Plate 8). If we consider what Grant Tavinor, a lecturer in
philosophy and also a gamer, said about his personal experience

of this game, it is clear that *BioShock*'s developers hit the spot: "I couldn't bring myself to harvest the Little Sister; in fact, the prospect of doing so made me feel queasy. And so, I saved her, an action that was accompanied by a sudden swelling of the accompanying music and my own emotions." Tavinor went so far as to claim that the game foregrounds "considerations of freewill and morality."[23]

It is time to pause and ponder these matters in depth. A videogame is a closed system, its rules set from the beginning by its creators. Players navigate those rules to get through the game and arrive at its end. The end is predetermined, and no matter what the player does or chooses, there are no real consequences except the one decided by those who make videogames. If the player's avatar dies, he is (endlessly) resurrected to try the game again. If he harvests, if he does not harvest, the consequence is still the end of the game. The only "quirk" in *BioShock* is the slightly different tone of each ending. This is why Robert Jackson called the decision about harvesting or not harvesting a "forced choice." Any choice made by the player is "functional": it gets the player to the end of the game. Critics have acclaimed the player's "agency" in *BioShock*, and, as we have seen, Tavenor acclaimed its moral value, but Jackson's observations undermine such praise: the game is a constructed system utterly controlled by its makers, not its players. Jackson asks: "How does one decide, let alone interpret, intervene or change a system where a player's actions are always already decided in advance during play?" To the claim of *BioShock*'s creator, Ken Levine, that he "gave control to the player," Jackson's reply is decisive: "Crucially Levine and the game designers find themselves in a precarious position: they give control to the player, without the player having any tangible freedom to choose."[24]

The videogame creators' real control reflects their politics and ideals. It extends to the emotions expressed in games and invoked in players. The small stock of feelings made available to the player unwittingly reveal the creators' own limited emotional imagination. We mean this not as a critique so much as a *liberating* suggestion. In an interview, Ken Levine remarked, "I am born with a depressive, anxious *brain*. So I'm full of regret. I use regret to say, 'How can I do it better in the future?'" The assumptions about emotions here – that they are in the brain, that they are simple, that they lead to action – are those of cognitivist theorists. They are presentist and universalist.[25]

But why should they be otherwise? It is because games are not *just* games. Like children's books, the emotions that they describe and invoke give us models for thinking about, understanding, and feeling our emotions. *The limitations of those models are our own.* Right now, we are being taught that there is a "normal," "correct" way to express the emotions that we feel. Those emotions are given simple labels: happiness, fear, anger, and so on. Out of the welter of feelings that we have – all their ambivalences, emotives, and histories – we are learning to choose *one* expression and to think of ourselves as feeling *one* way. It hurts us to be so limited in our repertories and comprehensions.

In her recent book on the brain's "secret life," neuro-psychologist Lisa Feldman Barrett challenges the "classical view" that emotions are universal, that they are hard-wired reflexes, that each is caused by a particular circuit in the brain, and so on. "We need a new theory of what emotions are and where they come from."[26] As Barrett counts on science, so we look to the *history* of emotions to reveal their "secret life." We know that emotions contain within them past, present, and future meanings; they are no one thing (there is no one "anger," no one "fear"); they are expressed not just "through bodies" (as Darwin was already saying) but through bodily practices that become habits over time; they are different for different communities; and so on.

Let us be blunt. We believe it is time to revolutionize the way we think of our emotional lives. It is time for educators, politicians, religious leaders, parents, and media creators to consider the history of emotions. They are the people who transmit knowledge, consensus, and advice about the human condition and society. This is not theoretical; it has everything to do with our practical lives. When our friend says, "I am happy," we need not expect his face to light up with a smile. In turn, if our friend smiles without uttering a word, we cannot simply infer that he is happy. We know that his happiness – even its announcement – is a relatively new phenomenon tied to modern social expectations. We know that its older meaning of economic independence lives on within it, as do older notions of heavenly felicity. We expect that his happiness is not unalloyed – that it is part of a larger sequence of feelings that our friend may announce in due course, or keep to himself. We also know that our full understanding of this happiness depends on how our friend is accustomed to express his feelings; how it is part of his repertory of practices. Likewise, when our child says, "I am unhappy," we do not ask her to frown; we do not imagine that her term "unhappiness" is the end of the story; we know that her tears may give her more pain and yet also offer pleasure; we expect that she will express other feelings by and by. And when we are in love, when our bodies yearn to touch – and yet fear to touch – our beloved, we know that within all the expectations of that yearning is the long history of love's many meanings. Within our love is its ancient association with lust, sacrifice, and romantic ideas of love's exclusivity. We are not surprised when love is accompanied by anger or fear or melancholy, or even seeming indifference.

We all know how powerful, deep, and complicated our feelings are. The history of emotions helps us see why and how. As it becomes diffused into the very ways in which we understand and live our emotions daily, it may also help us take better care of the ones that trouble us.

Conclusion

"At the end of the day, most people gotta put on a mask. Only in acting do people literally take it off."

Viola Davis, quoted in John Lahr, "Act of Grace," *New Yorker* (December 19 and 26, 2016), 64.

We have claimed that our own emotional lives will improve or at least become more understandable and pleasurable in the light of the history of emotions. Even so, the nagging question remains: are historians of emotion talking about *real* emotions when they plumb their sources? Can they say anything valid about emotional experience?

In a letter of 1762 to his friend and Virginia politician John Page, Thomas Jefferson recounted with some humor his many woes: rats had eaten his pocketbook, and a leak in the roof of his house had flooded his watch and destroyed the portrait of a young woman with whom he was more or less in love. Summing up, he asked: "Is there any such thing as happiness in this world? No." This from the man who thirteen years later was to write that the pursuit of happiness was the inalienable right of humankind! Are we doomed to think that Jefferson's "unhappiness" in the letter, not to mention his "happiness" in the Declaration, were not "real" emotions?[1]

What makes an emotion real or unreal? Today we have various "tests" to determine "authenticity." The TV show "Lie to Me" drew on Paul Ekman's work to claim that a person's face revealed his or her true feelings. Some scientists claim that fMRI scans of the brain tell us where emotions are located. Heart rate and skin conductance tests are said to betray emotions. However valid these signs of emotion may be, none *is* an emotion. In that sense, they are like words, which, again, are about emotions but are not emotions themselves. Furthermore, as we have seen, no emotion is one thing but carries in its train all sorts of possibilities, including their seeming opposites. When Viola Davis said that only in acting do people take off their masks, she was claiming, in effect, that make-believe is where emotions are most real. Even though we live in an age obsessed with questions of authenticity and sincerity, we will never know whether an emotion is real. Asking that question takes us nowhere.

Historians cannot scan the brains nor measure the skin conductance of their subjects, and even if they could, they would not see "a real emotion." But historians *can* interrogate contexts. In the case of happiness, they can gather other examples of the idea or, rather, the concept – the word filled with all its ramifications and meanings – in a given period. We have already briefly looked at happiness in Jefferson's milieu. Here is La Comtessa de Dia, a poet and musician writing around the 1180s:

> True joy gives me gladness
> And makes me sing more merrily.[2]

Should we believe that her "true joy" is real? She says explicitly that it is. Nevertheless, we should consider her reasons for declaring this: she wants to entertain us; she wants to impress us with her poetic skills; she wants to find patrons. We cannot say if her joy is real or unreal *for her*. But since we can read other poets and musicians as well as theologians and philosophers (and less exalted writings as well) from La Comtessa's time and place, we may very certainly say that she and her contemporaries, like us, imagined that there was something like "true joy," that people could feel it, and that, while it might not be expressed in a smile, it *was* thought to be expressed at times in merry songs. Thus, we can say a great deal about La Comtessa's emotion, even as the issue of "real" becomes a dead end.

Even if we see only the fugitive effects of emotions, nevertheless we know that they exist – and are powerful. If they are difficult to study, that is because they are so many things: practices, ways of communicating, ways of persuading, determinants of action, determinants of thought, and more. These are things historians study very well. Yet, medievalist Rüdiger Schnell claims that studying emotions historically is a contradiction in terms. For him, emotions exist only in the living and therefore must be the province of specialists – psychologists, neurophysiologists, sociologists, and philosophers – who work with "flesh-and-blood" people. Historical sources (says Schnell) are too limited to get at "real" emotions.[3]

This makes no sense. Any source and any study of emotions – whether about the past or the present – is limited when the goal is to access "real" feelings. That is because, like the Higgs boson, emotions are known by others only indirectly. We know (or think we know) how we feel. But how can others know our feelings if not obliquely? The boson reveals itself in all matter (that's why it was theorized in the first place), but its existence is ascertained only when it turns into other particles. Emotions disclose themselves through thoughts, bodily changes, words, practices, and acts. All of these have been the subject of historical studies, and all have shed light on the topic.

Furthermore, as this book has been at pains to show, we cannot really understand our own emotions *without* their history. The history of emotions has offered new ways to approach, assess, and even define them. The emotionological approach to fear helped explain post-9/11 security and surveillance practices in the United States. The notion of emotional refuge gave us a new way to understand the causes and eventual results of the French Revolution. Emotional communities brought a new way to see the emergence of the Levellers in seventeenth-century England, who drew on the emotions and practices of radical Protestant churches for a political program that emphasized freedom and happiness. Performatives made sense of behaviors that previously had been assessed as "impulsive." If there is one answer to "What Is the History of Emotions?" it must be that it is an ongoing discussion about the multiple ways in which emotions have played – and continue to play – a role in the unfolding drama of human history and in our own lives.

This does not mean that there are no problems or challenges ahead. But in this conclusion we wish to summarize what the field has achieved. In the wake of new psychological theories of the emotions that stress their social and cognitive origins, some historians began to create new sorts of histories that analyzed societies and their changes via the lenses of emotional standards, emotional regimes, emotional communities, and emotional performances. The first three tended to privilege written sources over other sorts of historical evidence, and they looked at words – of advice, strictures, and norms – more than at bodies. But the fourth, while relying on written texts, nevertheless stressed the role of bodies (particularly the bodies of rulers) in expressing emotions and therewith maintaining political control.

Soon many historians chafed at the emphasis on written texts and words. They became interested in the body as it confronted physicians, dealt with pain, or played out its gender. Some did not deny the importance of words, but they wanted historians to gather other sorts of materials and, on their basis, imaginatively consider how bodies were involved in producing the words, the gestures that accompanied them, and the performances that they implied. Others added the uses of space to the mix, asking historians to think about the meanings of places and spaces in creating, shaping, and expressing emotions. Still others, convinced by affect theory, thought it might be possible for historians to do without words altogether, relying simply on the impact of a space. Most recently, historians have explored how, when words do not exist or hardly exist, objects themselves may be considered "bodies" that interact with other (human) bodies on an emotional level. Some employ texts even if their emphasis is on the image. Others place objects in their larger cultural contexts to document the emotions that they express and evoke.

The general thrust of the field is – and should be – to dethrone binaries. One of those is the rift between scientists and historians, a rift hardly conceivable, for scholars in the arts and sciences are mutually interested in the origins and meanings of emotions. When psychological constructionists talk about conceptualizations, they are thinking about the biological effects of the ambient historical context. Another binary appeals to practices rather than texts, as if they may be separated. It should be evident from this book that the history of emotions has depended on texts (in general, the approaches surveyed in Chapter 2) and reacted against that reliance (as in Chapter 3). Nevertheless, when Rosenwein talked about the "joyous advent" of the ruler into the cities of the Duchy of Burgundy in the fifteenth century, she treated it as a "practice" meant to generate joy; and when Scheer described the "bodily practices" of English Methodists in the eighteenth century, she looked largely at texts, as for example the sermons of John Wesley, to discover those practices. Both gestures and words are, in the end, products of culture; future historians need not – had better not – choose one over the other. Similarly, material culture can never be divorced from its context: someone made the object, someone used it, someone was affected by it. If the object still exists, it is nevertheless not exactly what it was, nor is its meaning the same. Interpreting the object or the text requires similar efforts and questions. Just as concepts such as "male" and "female" are being problematized and transcended, so too "words" and "bodies" should not be essentialized. Both are forms of speech at the same time as they are forms of practice. Similarly, psychologists and historians of emotions are trying hard to move beyond another binary: the mind–body dualism, so ingrained in our culture. It is exceptionally durable in part because of its numerous guises, which include making reason the opposite of emotion, intention the contrary of automaticity, restraint incompatible with impulse. These oppositions seem natural because they are embedded in our very grammar. However, we must not imagine that the cure for dualism is always holism. The relationship between body and mind, emotion and reason, may be far more complicated. Curie Virág points out that in China during the Warring States period (475 to 221 BCE), emotions were understood to be *different from* cognition, and yet essential to achieving it. Moreover, the body – more particularly the heart – was the "site of both cognition and feelings." In mainstream Chinese thought of the period, "we find a tension between these two functions, but also a recognition that the highest level of ethical attainment involves their harmonization." In the thirteenth-century West, scholastic theologian Thomas Aquinas, too, thought that emotions were necessary for the perfection of virtue. These thinkers were not talking about holism but rather about connections and continuities.[4]

The field is moving beyond the distinctions that separate texts, practices, bodies, objects, and spaces. Emotions overlap boundaries, spilling into and out of our lives at every juncture, changing forms yet clinging to old habits over time. Revealing this complexity is the task of the history of emotions, but the lessons of that history are for everyone.

Notes

Introduction

1   The most important earlier survey of the field is Jan Plamper, *The History of Emotions: An Introduction*, trans. Keith Tribe (Oxford, 2015). Researchers of the early modern period now have Susan Broomhall, ed., *Early Modern Emotions: An Introduction* (London, 2017).

2   Readers interested in a philosophical approach to emotions might well begin with Robert C. Solomon, *The Passions* (Garden City, NY, 1976) and with his more recent edited collection, *Thinking About Feeling: Contemporary Philosophers on Emotions* (Oxford, 2004); for an anthropological approach, a classic is Catherine A. Lutz, *Unnatural Emotions: Everyday Sentiments on a Micronesian Atoll and Their Challenge to Western Theory* (Chicago, 1988); for a literary approach, see Gail Kern Paster, Katherine Rowe, and Mary Floyd-Wilson, eds, *Reading the Early Modern Passions: Essays in the Cultural History of Emotion* (Philadelphia, 2004).

3   For Shakespeare's will, see http://blog.nationalarchives.gov.uk/blog/shakespeares-will-new-interpretation.

1   Science

1   On some important distinctions in the meanings of words eventually subsumed under the term "emotion," see Claudia Wassmann, "Forgotten Origins, Occluded Meanings: Translation of Emotion Terms," *Emotion Review* 9/2 (2017): 163–71.

2   Aristotle, *Rhetoric* 2.1.8 (1378a), 2.2 (1378b), in Aristotle, *The "Art" of Rhetoric*, trans. John Henry Freese (London, 1926), 173. For more on Aristotle's theory, see David Konstan, *The Emotions of the Ancient Greeks* (Toronto, 2006).

3   Seneca, *On Anger* 2.1.4, quoted in Margaret R. Graver, *Stoicism and Emotion* (Chicago, 2007), 94.

4   Augustine, *The City of God* 14.6, quoted in Barbara H. Rosenwein, *Generations of Feeling: A History of Emotions, 600–1700* (Cambridge, 2016), 31.

5   On these developments, see Thomas Dixon, *From Passions to Emotions: The Creation of a Secular Psychological Category* (Cambridge, 2003). See also Otniel E. Dror, Bettina Hitzer, Anja Lauötter, and Pilar León-Sanz, eds, *History of Science and the Emotions = Osiris* 31 (2016).

6   Paul R. Kleinginna, Jr., and Anne M. Kleinginna, "A Categorized List of Emotion Definitions, with Suggestions for a Consensual Definition," *Motivation and Emotion* 5/4 (1981): 345–79, at 355.

7   For a consideration of the place of emotions in psychoanalysis, see Jorge Canestri, "Emotions in the Psychoanalytic Theory," in *From the Couch to the Lab: Trends in Psychodynamic Neuroscience*, ed. Aikaterini Fotopoulou, Donald Pfaff, and Martin A. Conway (Oxford, 2012), 176–85.

8   Randolph R. Cornelius, *The Science of Emotions: Research and Tradition in the Psychology of Emotion* (Upper Saddle River, 1996), 1.

9   See Rosenwein, *Generations of Feeling* on all these meanings of affects. On Aelred of Rievaulx's notion of affect, see Damien Boquet, "Affectivity in the Spiritual Writings of Aelred of Rievaulx," in *A Companion to Aelred of Rievaulx (1110–1167)*, ed. Marsha L. Dutton (Leiden, 2017), 167–96.

10 Charles Darwin, *The Expression of the Emotions in Man and Animals* (New York, 1898 [orig. publ. 1872]), 280–1.

11 G.-B. Duchenne de Boulogne, *The Mechanism of Human Facial Expression*, ed. and trans. R. Andrew Cuthbertson (Cambridge, 1990).

12 The original study was Paul Ekman and Wallace V. Friesen, "Constants across Cultures in the Face and Emotion," *Journal of Personality and Social Psychology* 17 (1971): 124–9. They added contempt in "A New Pan-Cultural Facial Expression of Emotion," *Motivation and Emotion* 10 (1986): 159–68. In the 1990s Ekman wrote a number of articles defending the concept of "basic emotions," culminating in his retrospective article "Basic Emotions," in *Handbook of Cognition and Emotion*, ed. Tim Dalgleish and Mick J. Power (Chichester, 1999), 45–60, where (at 55) he listed amusement, anger, contempt, contentment,

disgust, embarrassment, excitement, fear, guilt, pride in achieve ment, relief, sadness/distress, satisfaction, sensory pleasure, and shame. He did not connect all of these to a facial expression per se but rather (at 47) to a variety of "distinctive universal signals."

13 See http://www.paulekman.com/micro-expressions.

14 E. Richard Sorenson, *The Edge of the Forest: Land, Childhood and Change in a New Guinea Protoagricultural* Society (Washington, DC, 1976), 140; James A. Russell, "Is There Universal Recognition of Emotion from Facial Expression? A Review of the Cross-Cultural Studies," *Psychological Bulletin* 114 (1994): 102–41; Russell, "The Contempt Expression and the Relativity Thesis," *Motivation and Emotion* 15/2 (1991): 149–68; Ruth Leys, "How Did Fear Become a Scientific Object and What Kind of Object Is It?" *Representations* 110 (2008): 66–104, at 88. Most recently, see Carlos Crivelli, James A. Russell, Sergio Jarillo, and Jose-Miguel Fernandez-Dols, "Recognizing Spontaneous Facial Expressions of Emotion in a Small-Scale Society of Papua New Guinea," *Emotion* 17/2 (2017): 337–47, showing that spontaneous facial expressions from one group of indigenous residents were not interpreted according to Ekman's predictions by another such group.

15 Taylor J. Keding and Ryan J. Herringa, "Paradoxical Prefrontal-Amygdala Recruitment to Angry and Happy Expressions in Pediatric Posttraumatic Stress Disorder," *Neuropsychopharmacology* 41 (2016): 2903–12. Examples of the faces used are in a separate document, Supplemental Material, 9 (see Supplemental Figure 1).

16 Sebastian Jongen, Nikolai Axmacher, Nico A. W. Kremers, et al., "An Investigation of Facial Emotion Recognition Impairments in Alexithymia and its Neural Correlates," *Behavioural Brain Research* 271 (2014): 129–39.

17 William James, *Principles of Psychology* (Cambridge, 1890), 2:446–85, online at http://psychclassics.yorku.ca/James/Principles/prin25.htm, at 452. Italics in the original. William James, "What is an Emotion?" *Mind* 9 (1884): 188–205, at 189–90, online at http://psychclassics.yorku.ca/James/emotion.htm. Italics and small caps in the original.

18 James, "What is an Emotion?" 192; James, *Principles*, 448.

19 For a collection of articles summing up the legacy of Jamesian theory and its importance today, see *Emotion Review* 6/1 (2014): 3–52. A. R. Damasio, T. J. Grabowski, A. Bechara, et al., "Subcortical and Cortical Brain Activity during the Feeling of Self-Generated Emotions," *Nature Neuroscience* 3/10 (2000): 1049–2000.

20   Magda B. Arnold, *Emotion and Personality*, vol. 1: *Psychological Aspects* (New York, 1960), 171. Agnes Moors, Phoebe C. Ellsworth, Klaus R. Scherer, and Nico H. Frijda, "Appraisal Theories of Emotion: State of the Art and Future Development," *Emotion Review* 5/2 (2013): 119–24 provides a survey of the field.

21   Klaus R. Scherer, Marcel R. Zentner, and Daniel Stern, "Beyond Surprise: The Puzzle of Infants' Expressive Reactions to Expectancy Violation," *Emotion* 4/4 (2004): 389–402, at 389, 398. See also Kevin N. Ochsner, "How Thinking Controls Feeling: A Social Cognitive Neuroscience Approach," *Emotion* 4/4 (2004): 106–36.

22   Moors, Ellsworth, Scherer, and Frijda, "Appraisal Theories," 121; David Sander, Jordan Grafman, and Tiziana Zalla, "The Human Amygdala: An Evolved System for Relevance Detection," *Reviews in the Neurosciences* 14 (2003): 303–16.

23   Silvan S. Tomkins, "Affect Theory," in *Approaches to Emotion*, ed. Klaus R. Scherer and Paul Ekman (Hillsdale, NJ, 1984), 163–95, at 165. The list is simplified here; in the original, Tomkins coupled each affect to reflect different degrees of affective "activation." An example is fear/terror.

24   Tomkins, "Affect Theory," 163–4.

25   Tomkins, "Affect Theory," 145.

26   Tomkins, "Affect Theory," 168, 170, 175, 178, 180.

27   Jaak Panksepp, "The Affective Brain and Core Consciousness: How Does Neural Activity Generate Emotional Feelings?" in *Handbook of Emotions*, ed. Michael Lewis, Jeannette M. Haviland-Jones, and Lisa Feldman Barrett, 3rd edn (New York, 2008), 48; Nancy L. Stein, Marc W. Hernandez, and Tom Trabasso, "Advances in Modeling Emotion and Thought: The Importance of Developmental, Online, and Multilevel Analyses," in *Handbook of Emotions*, 574–86, at 578. Many other psychologists use "emotion" and "affect" interchangeably. Consider Alice M. Isen, "Some Ways in Which Positive Affect Influences Decision Making and Problem Solving," in *Handbook of Emotions*, 548–73, at 548: "Understanding of emotion and the role that common, everyday mild affect (feelings, emotion) play in people's thinking and behavior is still relatively rudimentary."

28   David Sander and Klaus R. Scherer, eds, *The Oxford Companion to Emotion and the Affective Sciences* (Oxford, 2009), 9–11, at 9–10.

29   For the beginning of social constructionism, see Peter L. Berger and Thomas Luckmann, *The Social Construction of Reality: A Treatise in the Sociology of Knowledge* (Garden City, NY, 1966). For sociology and emotions, see Jonathan H. Turner and Jan E. Stets, *The Sociology of Emotions* (Cambridge, 2005);

Eduardo Bericat, "The Sociology of Emotions: Four Decades of Progress," *Current Sociology* 64/3 (2016): 491–513. For anthropology, see Lutz, *Unnatural Emotions*.

30 Rom Harré, ed., *The Social Construction of Emotions* (Oxford, 1986), vii. Fully half of the contributors were in psychology departments, with most of the others in either philosophy or anthropology; James R. Averill, "The Acquisition of Emotions during Adulthood," in *The Social Construction of Emotions*, 98–119, at 100. On happiness, see Anna Wierzbicka, *Emotions across Languages and Cultures: Diversity and Universals* (Cambridge, 1999), 51–4; Barbara H. Rosenwein, "Emotion Keywords," in *Transitional States: Cultural Change, Tradition and Memory in Medieval Literature and Culture*, ed. Graham D. Caie and Michael D. C. Drout (Tempe, AZ, 2017), 33–51.

31 This idea may be traced to the work of sociologist and anthropologist Pierre Bourdieu, *Outline of a Theory of Practice* (Cambridge, 1977 [orig. publ. in French, 1972]).

32 See J. L. Austin, *How to Do Things with Words: The William James Lectures delivered at Harvard University in 1955* (Oxford, 1962).

33 Solomon, *The Passions*, 196, 199.

34 Arlie Hochschild, *The Managed Heart: Commercialization of Human Feeling* (Berkeley, 2012 [orig. publ. 1979]).

35 Lisa Feldman Barrett and James A. Russell, eds, *The Psychological Construction of Emotion* (New York, 2015), 86, 101–2.

36 Some neuroscientists not particularly concerned with emotions also "deconstruct" the older view of brain structures. See Larry W. Swanson and Gorica D. Petrovich, "What is the Amygdala?" *Trends in Neurosciences* 21 (1998): 323–31, at 323: "The amygdala is neither a structural nor a functional unit."

37 *Psychological Construction*, 116.

38 *Psychological Construction*, 63, 86, 89.

39 Adrian Bird, "Perceptions of Epigenetics," *Nature* 447 (2007): 396–98 gives an introduction to the topic.

40 Ian C. G. Weaver, Nadia Cervoni, Frances A. Champagne, et al., "Epigenetic Programming by Maternal Behavior," *Nature Neuroscience* 7/8 (2004): 847–54, at 847. Stress is here measured by HPA (Hypothalamic-Pituitary-Adrenal axis) responses. The possible mechanisms through which the programming occurs, involving an alteration in hippocampal glucocorticoid receptor expression, are explored in Ian C. G. Weaver, "Epigenetic Programming by Maternal Behavior and Pharmacological Intervention. Nature Versus Nurture: Let's Call the Whole Thing Off," *Epigenetics* 2/1 (2007): 22–8.

41 Siddhartha Mukherjee, *The Gene: An Intimate History* (New York, 2016), esp. 393–410, at 403, 405.

42   Daniel Lord Smail, *On Deep History and the Brain* (Berkeley, 2008), 150. On human–animal analogues, see Judith M. Stern, "Offspring-Induced Nurturance: Animal-Human Parallels," *Developmental Psychobiology* 31/1 (1997): 19–37, arguing that offspring elicit maternal responses in both animals and man, and referring to these as "emotional reactions to stimuli from offspring."

2   Approaches

1   Johan Huizinga, *The Autumn of the Middle Ages*, trans. Rodney J. Payton and Ulrich Mammitzsch (Chicago, 1996 [orig. publ. in Dutch, 1919]), 9. Criticizing the idea of primitive societies is Adam Kuper, *The Invention of Primitive Society: Transformations of an Illusion* (London, 1988).

2   Lucien Febvre, "Sensibility and History: How to Reconstitute the Emotional Life of the Past," in *A New Kind of History: From the Writings of Febvre*, ed. Peter Burke, trans. K. Folca (London, 1973 [orig. publ. in French, 1941]), 12–26, at 26. On the *Annales* school, see Carole Fink, *Marc Bloch: A Life in History* (Cambridge, 1989).

3   Norbert Elias, *The Civilizing Process*, trans. Edmund Jephcott, ed. Eric Dunning, Johan Goudsblom and Stephen Mennell, rev. edn (Oxford, 2000 [orig. publ. in German, 1939]), 241.

4   H. Norman Gardiner, Ruth Clark Metcalf, and John Gilbert Beebe-Center, *Feeling and Emotion: A History of Theories* (New York, 1937); Carla Casagrande and Silvana Vecchio, *Passioni dell'anima. Teorie e usi degli affetti nella cultura medievale* (Florence, 2015). For emotions' theory and "lived" emotions together, see Jan Plamper, "Fear: Soldiers and Emotion in Early Twentieth-Century Russian Military Psychology," *Slavic Review* 68/2 (2009): 259–83; Frank Biess and Daniel M. Gross, *Science and Emotions after 1945: A Transatlantic Perspective* (Chicago, 2014); Damien Boquet and Piroska Nagy, *Sensible Moyen Âge. Une histoire des émotions dans l'Occident médiéval* (Paris, 2015), and Rosenwein, *Generations of Feeling*.

5   Ludwig Janus, "Transformations in Emotions Structures Throughout History," *Journal of Psychohistory* 43/3 (2016): 187–99, at 189, 193; Lyndal Roper, *Oedipus and the Devil: Witchcraft, Sexuality and Religion in Early Modern Europe* (London, 1994).

6   Plamper, *History of Emotions*, 40–59 begins the modern historiography with the nineteenth century and is especially strong on German-language contributions; Damien Boquet and Piroska

Nagy, "Una storia diversa delle emozioni," *Rivista Storia d Ituli una* 128/2 (2016): 481–520 give the French bibliography. The *Annales* school notion of *mentalité* was important everywhere. An example in Italian historiography is Vito Fumagalli, *Landscapes of Fear: Perceptions of Nature and the City in the Middle Ages*, trans. Shayne Mitchell (Cambridge, 1994 [orig. publ. in Italian, 1987–90]), and in German studies is Peter Dinzelbacher, *Angst im Mittelalter: Teufels-, Todes- und Gotteserfahrung: Mentalitätsgeschichte und Ikonographie* (Paderborn, 1996).

7   Peter N. Stearns and Carol Z. Stearns, "Emotionology: Clarifying the History of Emotions and Emotional Standards," *American Historical Review* 90/4 (1985): 813–36, at 813.

8   Carol Zisowitz Stearns and Peter N. Stearns, *Anger: The Struggle for Emotional Control in America's History* (Chicago, 1986).

9   Stearns and Stearns, *Anger*, 71, 83, 93, 96–97.

10   Peter N. Stearns and Timothy Haggerty, "The Role of Fear: Transitions in American Emotional Standards for Children, 1850–1950," *American Historical Review* 96/1 (1991): 63–94, at 66.

11   Peter N. Stearns, *American Fear: The Causes and Consequences of High Anxiety* (New York, 2006), 31, 61.

12   Inger-Lise Lien, "Violence and Emotions," in *Pathways to Gang Involvement and Drug Distribution: Social, Environmental, and Psychological Factors* (Cham, 2014), 87–92, at 95.

13   Susan J. Matt, *Homesickness: An American History* (Oxford, 2011), 7; Ute Frevert, Pascal Eitler, Stephanie Olsen, et al., *Learning How to Feel: Children's Literature and Emotional Socialization, 1870–1970* (Oxford, 2014); Peter N. Stearns, *Satisfaction Not Guaranteed: Dilemmas of Progress in Modern Society* (New York, 2012), 2, 6.

14   Susan Matt and Peter N. Stearns, eds, *Doing Emotions History* (Urbana, 2014), 45.

15   William M. Reddy, "Against Constructionism: The Historical Ethnography of Emotions," *Current Anthropology* 38 (1997): 327–51, at 327.

16   William M. Reddy, *The Navigation of Feeling: A Framework for the History of Emotions* (Cambridge, 2001), 128. For the affect theory that most influenced Reddy, see Alice M. Isen and Gregory Andrade Diamond, "Affect and Automaticity," in *Unintended Thought: Limits of Awareness, Intention and Control*, ed. J. S. Uleman and John A. Bargh (New York, 1989), 124–52.

17   Reddy, "Against Constructionism," 335; Reddy, *Navigation of Feeling*, 129.

18   Reddy, *Navigation of Feeling*, 145.

19   Reddy, *Navigation of Feeling*, 217, 252.

20 William M. Reddy, *The Making of Romantic Love: Longing and Sexuality in Europe, South Asia, and Japan, 900–1200 CE* (Chicago, 2012).

21 Ferdiansyah Thajib, "Navigating Inner Conflict – Online Circulation of Indonesian Muslim Queer Emotions," in *Feelings at the Margins: Dealing with Violence, Stigma and Isolation in Indonesia,* ed. Thomas Stodulka and Birgitt Röttger-Rössler (Frankfurt, 2014), 159–79.

22 Valérie de Courville Nicol, *Social Economies of Fear and Desire: Emotional Regulation, Emotion Management, and Embodied Autonomy* (New York, 2011), 154.

23 Nicole Eustace, *Passion Is the Gale: Emotion, Power, and the Coming of the American Revolution* (Chapel Hill, 2008), 3, 110, 153.

24 Barbara H. Rosenwein, "Worrying about Emotions in History," *American Historical Review* 107 (2002): 821–45, at 842.

25 William V. Harris, *Restraining Rage: The Ideology of Anger Control in Classical Antiquity* (Cambridge, 2001).

26 C. Stephen Jaeger, *The Origins of Courtliness: Civilizing Trends and the Formation of Courtly Ideals, 939–1210* (Philadelphia, 1985).

27 On this, see Rosenwein, *Generations of Feeling,* 3–4.

28 For Reddy's "emotional" vs "non-emotional," see the appendix to Reddy, *Navigation of Feeling.* For emotions as expressed in words, see Rosenwein, *Generations of Feeling,* 4; Wierzbicka, *Emotions across Languages;* Lutz, *Unnatural Emotions;* Thomas Dixon, "Emotion: History of a Keyword in Crisis," *Emotion Review* 4/4 (2012): 338–44; Ute Frevert, Monique Scheer, Anne Schmidt, et al., *Emotional Lexicons: Continuity and Change in the Vocabulary of Feeling 1700–2000* (Oxford, 2014).

29 Dixon, *From Passions to Emotions.* For non-Western conceptions, see papers in Damien Boquet and Piroska Nagy, eds, *Histoire intellectuelle des émotions, de l'Antiquité à nos jours = L'Atelier du Centre de recherche historique* 16 (2016), online at https://acrh.revues.org/6720.

30 Barbara H. Rosenwein, *Emotional Communities in the Early Middle Ages* (Ithaca, 2006).

31 Rosenwein, *Emotional Communities,* 67.

32 Rosenwein, *Generations of Feeling,* 275.

33 Jennifer Cole and Lynn M. Thomas, *Love in Africa* (Chicago, 2009), 3, quoting Rosenwein, *Emotional Communities,* 191; Martha Tomhave Blauvelt, *The Work of the Heart: Young Women and Emotion, 1780–1830* (Charlottesville, 2007), 10; Joanne McEwan, " 'At My Mother's House,' Community and Household Spaces in Early Eighteenth-Century Scottish Infanticide

Narratives," in *Spaces for Feeling· Emotions and Sociabilities in Britain 1650–1850*, ed. Susan Broomhall (London, 2015), 12–34, at 21–3; Barbara Newman, *Making Love in the Twelfth Century: "Letters of Two Lovers" in Context* (Philadelphia, 2016), 26; Steven Mullaney, *The Reformation of Emotions in the Age of Shakespeare* (Chicago, 2015), 69.

34 Erving Goffman, *The Presentation of Self in Everyday Life* (New York, 1959); Clifford Geertz, *Negara: The Theater State in Nineteenth-Century Bali* (Princeton, 1980); Judith Butler, *Gender Trouble: Feminism and the Subversion of Identity*, 2nd edn (London, 1999). For historians, see Richard Wortman, *Scenarios of Power: Myth and Ceremony in Russian Monarchy*, 2 vols (Princeton, 1995–2000). For surveys of the "performative turn" see Peter Burke, "The Performative Turn in Recent Cultural history," in *Medieval and Early Modern Performance in the Eastern Mediterranean*, ed. Arzu Öztürkmen and Evelyn Birge Vitz (Turnhout, 2014), 541–61; Jürgen Martschukat and Steffen Patzold, eds, *Geschichtswissenschaft und "performative turn." Ritual, Inszenierung und Performanz vom Mittelalter bis zur Neuzeit* (Cologne, 2003).

35 For a review of the subject, see the essays in Stuart Airlie, Walter Pohl, and Helmut Reimitz, eds, *Staat im Frühen Mittelalter* (Vienna, 2006).

36 Gerd Althoff, "Empörung, Tränen, Zerknirschung. 'Emotionen' in der öffentlichen Kommunikation des Mittelalters," *Frühmittelalterliche Studien* 30 (1996): 60–79.

37 Althoff, "Empörung," 61, 63, 66. See also Althoff, *Otto III*, trans. Phyllis G. Jestice (University Park, 2002 [orig. publ. in German, 1996]), 112–18, 124–5.

38 Althoff, *Otto III*, 33.

39 J. E. A. Jolliffe, *Angevin Kingship* (New York, 1963); Gerd Althoff, "*Ira Regis*: Prolegomena to a History of Royal Anger," in *Anger's Past: The Social Uses of an Emotion in the Middle Ages*, ed. Barbara H. Rosenwein (Ithaca, 1998), 59–74, at 61.

40 Geoffrey Koziol, *Begging Pardon and Favor: Ritual and Political Order in Early Medieval France* (Ithaca, 1992).

41 Klaus Oschema, *Freundschaft und Nähe im spätmittelalterlichen Burgund. Studien zum Spannungsfeld von Emotion und Institution* (Cologne, 2006), 24.

42 Laurent Smagghe, *Les Émotions du prince. Émotion et discours politique dans l'espace bourguignon* (Paris, 2012), 23.

43 For ancient rhetoric, see Ed Sanders and Matthew Johncock, eds, *Emotion and Persuasion in Classical Antiquity* (Stuttgart, 2016); Doris Kolesch, *Theater der Emotionen. Ästhetik und Politik zur Zeit Ludwigs XIV* (Frankfurt, 2006).

4

44   C. Dallett Hemphill, "Class, Gender, and the Regulation of Emotional Expression in Revolutionary-Era Conduct Literature," in *An Emotional History of the United States*, ed. Peter N. Stearns and Jan Lewis (New York, 1998), 33–51, at 34, 37–8, 42.

45   Stearns, *Satisfaction* Not *Guaranteed*, 41–2.

46   Eustace, *Passion Is the Gale*, 5, 398.

47   Jan Lewis, *The Pursuit of Happiness: Family and Values in Jefferson's Virginia* (Cambridge, 1983), 108, 121. See also Pauline Maier, *American Scripture: Making the Declaration of Independence* (New York, 1997), 134, who argues that Jefferson substituted the single word "happiness" for a longer phrase that he knew from a draft of the Virginia Declaration of Rights, which said that among the rights of men were "the enjoyment of life and liberty, with the means of acquiring and possessing property, and pursuing and obtaining happiness and safety."

48   Eustace, *Passion Is the Gale*, 19.

49   All quotations are taken from the online version of Epistle 4 at http://www.gutenberg.org/files/2428/2428-h/2428-h.htm.

50   Phil Withington, "The Art of Medicine: Utopia, Health, and Happiness," *The Lancet* 387/10033 (2016): 2084–85, at 2085.

51   On the performative nature of documents, see Geoffrey Koziol, *The Politics of Memory and Identity in Carolingian Royal Diplomas: The West Frankish Kingdom (840–987)* (Turnhout, 2012), esp. 42–62; on the type of parchment and uses made of the Declaration in U.S. history, see Maier, *American Scripture*, xi; for Martin Luther King, Jr., "I Have a Dream" Speech, see http://www.ushistory.org/documents/i-have-a-dream.htm.

52   For rights language, Brian Tierney, *The Idea of Natural Rights: Studies on Natural Rights, Natural Law, and Church Law, 1150–1625* (Atlanta, 1997). John Locke, *Second Treatise of Government* (1690), 2.6–7, quoted from https://www.gutenberg.org/files/7370/7370-h/7370-h.htm and cited by chapter and section. For royal documents on behalf of colonists, see the many charters online at http://avalon.law.yale.edu/subject_menus/statech.asp.

53   James P. McClure and J. Jefferson Looney, eds, *The Papers of Thomas Jefferson Digital Edition* (Charlottesville, 2008–17), online at http://rotunda.upress.virginia.edu/founders/TSJN-01-01-02-0175.

54   Sara Martin, ed., *The Adams Papers Digital Edition* (Charlottesville, 2008–17), online at http://rotunda.upress.virginia.edu/founders/ADMS-06-04-02-0142.

55   Reddy, *Navigation of Feeling*, 57; Rosenwein, *Generations of Feeling*, 316.

3   Bodies

1   Caroline Walker Bynum, "Why All the Fuss about the Body? A Medievalist's Perspective," *Critical Inquiry* 22 (1995): 1–33, at 5.

2   Jacques Revel and Jean-Pierre Peter, "Le corps. L'homme malade et son histoire," in *Faire de l'histoire*, vol. 3: *Nouveaux objets*, ed. Jacques Le Goff and Pierre Nora (Paris, 1974), 169–91.

3   Danielle Jacquart and Claude Alexandre Thomasset, *Sexuality and Medicine in the Middle Ages*, trans. Matthew Adamson (Cambridge, 1988 [orig. publ. in French, 1985]); Thomas Laqueur, *Making Sex: Body and Gender from the Greeks to Freud* (Cambridge, 1992); Michel Foucault, *Discipline and Punish: The Birth of the Prison*, trans. Alan Sheridan (New York, 1979 [orig. publ. in French, 1975]), 25. See also Foucault, *The History of Sexuality*, trans. Robert Hurley: vol. 1, *An Introduction*; vol. 2, *The Use of Pleasure*; vol. 3, *The Care of the Self* (New York, 1978–86 [orig. publ. in French, 1976–84]).

4   Peter Brown, *The Body and Society: Men, Women and Sexual Renunciation in Early Christianity* (New York, 1988), xiii; Caroline Walker Bynum, *Holy Feast and Holy Fast: The Religious Significance of Food to Medieval Women* (Berkeley, 1987). Bynum continued her study of the body's cultural meanings in *The Resurrection of the Body in Western Christianity, 200–1336* (New York, 1995). Marcel Mauss, "Techniques of the body," *Economy and Society* 2/1 (1973): 70–88, at 70 [orig. publ. in French, 1935].

5   Otniel E. Dror, "Creating the Emotional Body: Confusion, Possibilities, and Knowledge," in *An Emotional History of the United States*, 173–94; Dror, "The Scientific Image of Emotion: Experience and Technologies of Inscription," *Configurations* 7 (1999): 355–401, at 401; see also Dror, "The Affect of Experiment: The Turn to Emotions in Anglo-American Physiology, 1900–1940," *Isis* 90 (1999): 205–37.

6   On the medical gaze, Michel Foucault, *The Birth of the Clinic: An Archaeology of Medical Perception* (New York, 1973 [orig. publ. in French, 1963]); on examination, see Foucault, *Discipline and Punish*, 192, on the Panopticon, *Discipline and Punish*, 195; on Dror's scientists, see esp. Dror, "Creating the Emotional Body," 177–8.

7   Fay Bound Alberti, *Medicine, Emotion and Disease, 1700–1950* (Basingstoke, 2006), xix.

8   Most of the quotations in this paragraph are from Fay Bound Alberti, *Matters of the Heart: History, Medicine, and Emotion*

(Oxford, 2010), 3–5, 58; for the American Heart Association website see http://www.heart.org/HEARTORG/Conditions/HeartAttack/DiagnosingaHeartAttack/Angina-Pectoris-Stable-Angina_UCM_437515_Article.jsp#.

9   Bound Alberti, *Matters of the Heart*, 8–9; Bound Alberti, *This Mortal Coil: The Human Body in History and Culture* (Oxford, 2016), 17; see also Bound Alberti, "Bodies, Hearts, and Minds: Why Emotions Matter to Historians of Science and Medicine," *Isis* 100/4 (2009): 798–810. On cardiomyopathy, see Jun-Won Lee and Byung-il William Choi, "Stress-induced Cardiomyopathy: Mechanism and Clinical Aspects," in *Somatization and Psychosomatic Symptoms*, ed. Kyung Bong Koh (New York, 2013), 191–206. They too use the case of John Hunter to underline the "close connection between brain and heart" (199–200).

10   Elena Carrera, ed., *Emotions and Health, 1200–1700* (Leiden, 2013), 1, 5, 9.

11   Jacques Gélis, "Le corps, l'Église et le sacré," in *Histoire du corps*, ed. Alain Corbin, Jean-Jacques Courtine, and Georges Vigarello, 3 vols (Paris, 2005–6), 1:54; Jan Frans van Dijkhuizen and Karl A. E. Enenkel, eds, *The Sense of Suffering: Constructions of Physical Pain in Early Modern Culture* (Leiden, 2008), 10 (emphasis in original).

12   Esther Cohen, *The Modulated Scream: Pain in Late Medieval Culture* (Chicago, 2010).

13   Boquet and Nagy, *Sensible Moyen Âge*; Jean Leclercq, *The Love of Learning and the Desire for God: A Study of Monastic Culture* (New York, 1961 [orig. publ. in French, 1957]).

14   Michael Schoenfeldt, "The Art of Pain Management in Early Modern England," in *Sense of Suffering*, 19–38, at 27.

15   Joanna Bourke, *The Story of Pain: From Prayer to Painkillers* (Oxford, 2014), 17, 19; see also Keith Wailoo, *Pain: A Political History* (Baltimore, 2014).

16   Javier Moscoso, *Pain: A Cultural History*, trans. Sarah Thomas and Paul House (New York, 2012 [orig. publ. in Spanish, 2011]), 6, 8; Elaine Scarry, *The Body in Pain* (Oxford, 1985).

17   Rob Boddice, "Introduction: Hurt Feelings?" in *Pain and Emotion in Modern History*, ed. Rob Boddice (Basingstoke, 2014), 1–15, at 3, 4–5.

18   For a useful introduction to gender history, see Sonya O. Rose, *What is Gender History?* (Cambridge, 2010) which, however, does not discuss emotions. For that, see Willemijn Ruberg, "Introduction," in *Sexed Sentiments: Interdisciplinary Perspectives on Gender and Emotion*, ed. Willemijn Ruberg and Kristine Steenbergh (Amsterdam, 2011), 1–20.

19 Stephanie A. Shields, "Functionalism, Darwinism, and the Psychology of Women: A Study in Social Myth," *American Psychologist* 30/7 (1975): 739–54, at 739.

20 Marsha E. Fingerer, "Psychological Sequelae of Abortion: Anxiety and Depression," *Journal of Community Psychology* 1 (1973): 221–5; M. Steiner and D. R. Aleksandrowicz, "Psychiatric Sequelae to Gynaecological Operations," *Israel Annals of Psychiatry and Related Disciplines* 8 (1970): 186–92; Eduardo Dallal y Castillo, E. Shapiro Ackerman, A. Fernández Flores, A. M. Pallares Díaz, and J. E. Soberanes Rosales, "Psychological Characteristics of a Group of Premenopausal Women as Outlined through Tests," *Neurologia, Neurocirugia, Psiquiatria* 16 (1975): 243–53. The figures offered here were obtained from searching the database PsycINFO.

21 Carroll Smith-Rosenberg, "The Female World of Love and Ritual: Relations between Women in Nineteenth-Century America," *Signs* 1/1 (1975): 1–29, at 4, 9; Sharon Marcus, *Between Women: Friendship, Desire, and Marriage in Victorian England* (Princeton, 2007).

22 John Boswell, *Same-sex Unions in Premodern Europe* (New York, 1994), x, xxv; C. Stephen Jaeger, *Ennobling Love: In Search of a Lost Sensibility* (Pennsylvania, 1999); Alan Bray, *The Friend* (Chicago, 2003), 4. Claudia Rapp, *Brother-Making in Late Antiquity and Byzantium: Monks, Laymen, and Christian Ritual* (Oxford, 2016), proposes a Byzantine monastic context for the origins of the rituals of union that Boswell and Bray document. They were blessings for a couple about to retreat into semi-eremitic life.

23 David F. Greenberg, *The Construction of Homosexuality* (Chicago, 1988); Joan W. Scott, "Gender: A Useful Category of Historical Analysis," *American Historical Review* 91/5 (1986): 1053–75; Butler, *Gender Trouble*. Agneta H. Fischer, "Sex Differences in Emotionality: Fact or Stereotype?" *Feminism and Psychology* 3 (1993): 303–18 argued that women's greater "emotionality" was a red herring. Stephanie A. Shields, "Thinking about Gender, Thinking about Theory: Gender and Emotional Experience," in *Gender and Emotion: Social Psychological Perspectives*, ed. Agneta H. Fischer (New York, 2000): 3–23, at 6–7; Penelope Gouk and Helen Hills, eds, *Representing Emotions: New Connections in the History of Art, Music, and Medicine* (Aldershot, 2005), 22.

24 Bynum, "Why All the Fuss about the Body?" esp. 6–8, 16–18; Christine Battersby, "The Man of Passion: Emotion, Philosophy, and Sexual Difference," in *Representing Emotions*, 139–53.

25   Piroska Nagy, *Le don des larmes au Moyen Âge. Un instrument spirituel en quête d'institution (V^e–XIIIe siècle)* (Paris, 2000); Ruth Mazo Karras, *From Boys to Men: Formations of Masculinity in Late Medieval Europe* (Philadelphia, 2003), 65; Bernard Capp, "'Jesus Wept' But Did the Englishman? Masculinity and Emotion in Early Modern England," *Past and Present* 224 (2014): 75–108, at 76; on the "man of feeling," see Julie Ellison, *Cato's Tears and the Making of Anglo-American Emotion* (Chicago, 1999) and G. J. Barker-Benfield, *The Culture of Sensibility: Sex and Society in Eighteenth-Century Britain* (Chicago, 1992), but also on the nineteenth-century battlefield in Holly Furneaux, *Military Men of Feeling: Emotion, Touch, and Masculinity in the Crimean War* (Oxford, 2016); on the emotions expressed in the First World War, Michael Roper, *The Secret Battle: Emotional Survival in the Great War* (Manchester, 2010); Joanna Bourke, *Dismembering the Male: Men's Bodies, Britain, and the Great War* (Chicago, 1996); on the fascist man, Sandro Bellassai, "The Masculine Mystique: Anti-modernism and Virility in Fascist Italy," *Journal of Modern Italian Studies* 10/3 (2005): 314–35; Gigliola Gori, "Model of Masculinity: Mussolini, the 'New Italian' of the Fascist Era," *The International Journal of the History of Sport* 16/4 (1999): 27–61.

26   Douglas Schrock and Brian Knop, "Gender and Emotions," in *Handbook of the Sociology of Emotions*, ed. Jan E. Stets and Jonathan H. Turner, 2 vols (Dordrecht, 2014), 2:411–28, at 412.

27   Stephanie Tarbin, "Raising Girls and Boys: Fear, Awe, and Dread in the Early Modern Household," in *Authority, Gender and Emotions in Late Medieval and Early Modern England*, ed. Susan Broomhall (London, 2015), 106–30; Annemarieke Willemsen, "'That the boys come to school half an hour before the girls': Order, Gender, and Emotion in School, 1300–1600," in *Gender and Emotions in Medieval and Early Modern Europe: Destroying Order, Structuring Disorder*, ed. Susan Broomhall (Farnham, 2015), 175–96; Merridee L. Bailey, *Socialising the Child in Late Medieval England, c. 1400–1600* (York, 2012). See also Claudia Jarzebowski and Thomas Max Safley, *Childhood and Emotion across Cultures, 1450–1800* (London, 2014) and Frevert, Eitler, Olsen, et al., *Learning How to Feel*.

28   Lawrence Stone, *The Family, Sex, and Marriage in England, 1500–1800* (New York, 1977), 93, 99; Emlyn Eisenach, *Husbands, Wives, and Concubines: Marriage, Family, and Social Order in Sixteenth-Century Verona* (Kirksville, 2004), 79.

29   Boquet and Nagy, *Sensible Moyen Âge*, 259.

30   Douglas Schrock, Daphne Holden, and Lori Reid, "Creating Emotional Resonance: Interpersonal Emotion Work and

Motivational Framing in a Transgender Community," *Social Problems* 51/1 (2004): 61–81; Stephanie L. Budge, Joe J. Orovecz, and Jayden L. Thai, "Trans Men's Positive Emotions: The Interaction of Gender Identity and Emotion Labels," *The Counseling Psychologist* 43/3 (2015): 404–34.

31 Caroline Walker Bynum, "Jesus as Mother and Abbot as Mother: Some Themes in Twelfth-Century Cistercian Writing," *Harvard Theological Review* 70 (1977): 257–84, at 262; Kathryn M. Ringrose, *The Perfect Servant: Eunuchs and the Social Construction of Gender in Byzantium* (Chicago, 2007), 31; see also Mathew Kuefler, *The Manly Eunuch: Masculinity, Gender Ambiguity, and Christian Ideology in Late Antiquity* (Chicago, 2001). For modern eunuchs and their gender identity, see Richard J. Wassersug, Emma McKenna, and Tucker Lieberman, "Eunuch as a Gender Identity after Castration," *Journal of Gender Studies* 21/3 (2012): 253–70.

32 Megan McLaughlin, *Sex, Gender, and Episcopal Authority in an Age of Reform, 1000–1122* (Cambridge, 2010), 121.

33 Michel Feher, "Introduction," in *Fragments for a History of the Human Body*, ed. Michel Feher, with Ramona Naddaff and Nadia Tazi, 3 vols (New York, 1989), 1:14; René Nelli, "Love's Rewards," in *Fragments for a History*, 2:219–35.

34 Monique Scheer, "Are Emotions a Kind of Practice (and Is That What Makes Them Have a History)? A Bourdieuian Approach to Understanding Emotion," *History and Theory* 51 (2012): 193–220, at 209, 217–18, 220.

35 See Pascal Eitler and Monique Scheer, "Emotionengeshichte als Körpergeschichte: Eine heuristische Perspektive auf religiöse Konversionen im 19. und 20. Jahrhundert," *Geschichte und Gesellschaft* 35 (2009): 282–313; Scheer, "Feeling Faith: The Cultural Practice of Religious Emotions in Nineteenth-Century German Methodism," in *Out of the Tower. Essays on Culture and Everyday Life*, ed. Monique Scheer, Thomas Thiemeyer, Reinhard Johler, and Bernhard Tschofer, trans. Michael Robertson (Tübingen, 2013), 217–47.

36 Margrit Pernau and Imke Rajamani, "Emotional Translations: Conceptual History beyond Language," *History and Theory* 55 (2016): 46–65, at 64. For bodies in film theory, see, for example, Christiane Voss, "Film Experience and the Formation of Illusion: The Spectator as 'Surrogate Body' for the Cinema," trans. Inga Pollmann, SCMS Translation Committee, intro. Vinzenz Hediger, *Cinema Journal* 50/4 (2011): 136–50; Jo Labanyi, "Doing Things: Emotion, Affect, and Materiality," *Journal of Spanish Cultural Studies* 11/3–4 (2010): 223–33, at 230.

37 Stephen Halliwell, *Greek Laughter: A Study of Cultural Psychology from Homer to Early Christianity* (Cambridge, 2008), viii–ix; Mary Beard, *Laughter in Ancient Rome: On Joking, Tickling, and Cracking Up* (Berkeley, 2014), x. For studies of gesture, see e.g. Gregory S. Aldrete, *Gestures and Acclamations in Ancient Rome* (Baltimore, 1999).

38 On the medieval laugh and invention of the smile, Jacques Le Goff, "Laughter in the Middle Ages," in *A Cultural History of Humour: From Antiquity to the Present Day*, ed. Jan Bremmer and Herman Roodenburg (Cambridge, 2005), 40–53; on the various meanings of medieval and early modern laughter, Albrecht Classen, ed., *Laughter in the Middle Ages and Early Modern Times: Epistemology of a Fundamental Human Behavior, its Meaning, and Consequences* (Berlin, 2010); on ancient Greek and Latin terms, see Beard, *Laughter in Ancient Rome*, 73–6; on the "smile revolution," Colin Jones, *The Smile Revolution in Eighteenth Century Paris* (Oxford, 2014); on laughter in the same period, Stéphanie Fournier, *Rire au théâtre à Paris à la fin du XVIIIe siècle* (Paris, 2016), 353; on the smile and the laugh, Colin Jones, "Le sourire," in *Histoire des Émotions*, ed. Alain Corbin, Jean-Jacques Courtine, and Georges Vigarello, vol. 1: *De l'Antiquité aux Lumières*, ed. Georges Vigarello (Paris, 2016), 446–59.

39 https://www.poetryfoundation.org/poems-and-poets/poems/detail/45937.

40 Sara Ahmed, *The Cultural Politics of Emotion*, 2nd edn (New York, 2015), 1; Bruce R. Smith, *Phenomenal Shakespeare* (Chichester, 2009), xviii.

41 Gregory J. Seigworth and Melissa Gregg, "An Inventory of Shimmers," in *The Affect Theory Reader* (Durham, 2010), 1–2; Stein, Hernandez, and Trabasso, "Advances in Modeling Emotion and Thought," 578–79; Brian Massumi, "The Autonomy of Affect," *Cultural Critique* 31 = *The Politics of Systems and Environments* pt. 2 (1995): 83–109, at 85.

42 Smith, *Phenomenal Shakespeare*, xvi, 45, 56, 62 (quoting Bulwer).

43 Douglas Barnett and Hilary Horn Ratner, "Introduction: The Organization and Integration of Cognition and Emotion in Development," *Journal of Experimental Child Psychology* 67 (1997): 303–16, at 303; Ruth Leys, "The Turn to Affect," *Critical Inquiry* 37 (2011): 434–72. For the reception of affect theory among historians, see Stephanie Trigg, "Introduction: Emotional Histories – Beyond the Personalization of the Past and the Abstraction of Affect Theory," *Exemplaria* 26 (2014): 3–15.

44 Seigworth and Gregg, *Affect Theory*, 3–4.

45 Henri Lefebvre, *The Production of Space* (Oxford, 1991 [orig. publ. in French, 1974]).

46 Margrit Pernau, "Space and Emotion: Building to Feel," *History Compass* 12/7 (2014): 541–9, at 545.

47 Ben Anderson, "Becoming and Being Hopeful: Towards a Theory of Affect," *Environment and Planning D: Society and Space* 24 (2006): 733–52, at 735–6 (emphasis in original).

48 Steve Pile, "Emotions and Affect in Recent Human Geography," *Transactions of the Institute of British Geographers* (n.s.) 35/1 (2010): 5–20, at 6.

49 Joyce Davidson and Christine Milligan, "Editorial. Embodying Emotion Sensing Space: Introducing Emotional Geographies," *Social and Cultural Geographies* 5/4 (2004): 523–32.

50 Benno Gammerl, "Emotional Styles – Concepts and Challenges," in *Rethinking History* 16/2 (2012): 161–75, at 161.

51 Andreas Reckwitz, "Affective Spaces: A Praxeological Outlook," in *Rethinking History* 16/2 (2012): 241–58, at 244, 247, 249, 256 (emphasis in original).

52 Mark Seymour, "Emotional Arenas: From Provincial Circus to National Courtroom in Late Nineteenth-Century Italy," in *Rethinking History* 16/2 (2012): 177–98, at 189–90, 193.

53 Tracy Adams, "Fostering Girls in Early Modern France," in *Emotions in the Household, 1200–1900*, ed. Susan Broomhall (London, 2008), 103–18, at 105, 113; Ivan Jablonka, "Fictive Kinship: Wards and Foster-Parents in Nineteenth-Century France," in *Emotions in the Household*, 269–84, at 273, 275.

54 Susan Broomhall, "Introduction," in *Spaces for Feeling*, 1–11, at 1.

55 Daniel Miller, *Material Culture and Mass Consumption* (Oxford, 1987); Miller, ed., *Materiality* (Durham, 2005); Arjun Appadurai, *The Social Life of Things: Commodities in Cultural Perspective* (Cambridge, 1989); Alfred Gell, *Art and Agency: An Anthropological Theory* (Oxford, 1998). For the Krems roundtable, see Barbara H. Rosenwein, "Emotions and Material Culture: A 'Site under Construction,'" in *Emotions and Material Culture*, ed. Gerhard Jaritz (Vienna, 2003), 165–72.

56 Sarah Tarlow, "Emotion in Archaeology," *Current Anthropology* 41/5 (2000): 713–46, at 723–5, 729.

57 Chris Gosden, "Aesthetics, Intelligence and Emotions: Implications for Archaeology," in *Rethinking Materiality: The Engagement of Mind with the Material World*, ed. Elizabeth Demarrais, Chris Gosden, and Colin Renfrew (Cambridge, 2004), 33–40, at 33, 37.

58 Oliver J. T. Harris and Tim Flohr Sørensen, "Rethinking Emotion and Material Culture," *Archaeological Dialogues* 17/2

(2010): 145–63, at 146, 148, 152, 155–6, 162. Sarah Tarlow, "The Archaeology of Emotion and Affect," *Annual Review of Anthropology* 41 (2012): 169–85, at 174, 181. Contra Harris and Sørensen, see John Kieschnick, "Material Culture," in *The Oxford Handbook of Religion and Emotion*, ed. John Corrigan (Oxford, 2008), 223–40, who stresses artists' conscious effort to affect people through their creations.

59   Sarah Tarlow, "Death and Commemoration," *Industrial Archaeology Review* 27/1 (2005): 163–9, at 164, 167; Rosenwein, *Emotional Communities*, 57–78; Angelos Chaniotis, "Moving Stones: The Study of Emotions in Greek Inscriptions," in *Unveiling Emotions: Sources and Methods for the Study of Emotions in the Greek World*, ed. Angelos Chaniotis (Stuttgart, 2012), 91–129; Chaniotis, "Emotions in Public Inscriptions of the Hellenistic Age," *Mediterraneo antico*, 16/2 (2013): 745–60; Jeffrey Jerome Cohen, *Stone: An Ecology of the Inhuman* (Minneapolis, 2015), 12.

60   Cohen, *Stone*, 13; Elina Gertsman, "The Facial Gesture: (Mis)reading Emotion in Gothic Art," *The Journal of Medieval Religious Cultures* 36 (2010): 28–46; Jacqueline E. Jung, "The Portal from San Vicente Martír in Frías: Sex, Violence, and the Comfort of Community in a Thirteenth-Century Sculpture Program at the Cloisters," in *Theologisches Wissen und die Kunst. Festschrift für Martin Büchsel*, ed. Rebecca Müller, Anselm Rau, and Johanna Scheel (Berlin, 2015), 369–82.

61   Catherine Richardson, "'A very fit hat': Personal Objects and Early Modern Affection," in *Everyday Objects: Medieval and Early Modern Material Culture and its Meanings*, ed. Tara Hamling and Catherine Richardson (Farnham, 2010), 289–98, at 293; Lena Cowen Orlin, "Empty Vessels," in *Everyday Objects*, 299–308, at 300, 303; Orlin does not, however, mention Shakespeare's will.

62   John Styles, "Objects of Emotion: The London Foundling Hospital Tokens, 1741–1760," in *Writing Material Culture History*, ed. Anne Gerritsen and Giorgio Riello (London, 2015), 165–72, at 166–68, 171. See also Styles, *Threads of Feeling: The London Foundling Hospital's Textile Tokens, 1740–1770* (London, 2010).

63   Tove Engelhardt Mathiassen, "Protective Strategies and Emotions Invested in Early Modern Danish Christening Garments," in *Emotional Textiles*, ed. Alice Dolan and Sally Holloway = *Textile: Cloth and Culture* 14/2 (2016): 208–25, at 211–12, 215. On public history, museum exhibits, and emotions, see Sheila Watson, "Emotions in the History Museum," in *International Handbooks of Museum Studies: Museum Theory*,

ed. Andrew Wirth and Kylie Jones (Houten, 2015), 283–301.

64   Sara Ahmed, "Happy Objects," in *Affect Theory*, 29–51, at 29, 35; Alice Dolan and Sally Holloway, "Emotional Textiles: An Introduction," in *Emotional Textiles*, 152–59; Cohen, *Stone*, 22, 96–97.

65   Daniel Lord Smail, "Enmity and the Distraint of Goods in Late Medieval Marseille," in *Emotions and Material Culture*, 17–30, at 21; Elizabeth Howie, "Bringing Out the Past: Courtly Cruising and Nineteenth-Century American Men's Romantic Friendship Portraits," in *Love Objects: Emotion, Design and Material Culture*, ed. Anna Moran and Sorcha O'Brien (London, 2014), 43–52; Ann Wilson, "Kitsch, Enchantment and Power: The Bleeding Statues of Templemore in 1920," in *Love Objects*, 87–98.

66   Rey Chow, "Fateful Attachments: On Collection, Fidelity, and Lao She," *Critical Inquiry* 18 (2001): 286–304; Daniel Lord Smail, "Neurohistory in Action: Hoarding and the Human Past," *Isis* 105/1 (2014): 110–22.

67   Martha C. Nussbaum, *Upheavals of Thought: The Intelligence of Emotions* (Cambridge, 2001), 241. Already Susan L. Feagin, *Reading with Feeling: The Aesthetics of Appreciation* (Ithaca, 1996) emphasized the emotional dimensions of reading. "Reader response" is an important aspect of current approaches to literature.

68   Marianne Noble, *The Masochistic Pleasures of Sentimental Literature* (Princeton, 2000), 4, 6.

69   Pascal Eitler, Stephanie Olsen, and Uffa Jensen, "Introduction," in *Learning How to Feel*, 17.

70   Jan Plamper, "Ivan's Bravery," in *Learning How to Feel*, 203; Sarah Bilston, " 'It is Not What We Read, But How We Read': Maternal Counsel on Girls' Reading Practices in Mid-Victorian Literature," *Nineteenth-Century Contexts* 30/1 (2008): 1–20, at 6–7, 9, 14.

71   Rachel Ablow, "Introduction," in *The Feeling of Reading: Affective Experience and Victorian Literature*, ed. Rachel Ablow (Ann Arbor, 2010), 1–10, at 1–2; Nicholas Dames, "On Not Close Reading: The Prolonged Excerpt as Victorian Critical Protocol," in *The Feeling of Reading*, 11–26, at 22; Kate Flint, "Traveling Readers," in *The Feeling of Reading*, 27–46.

72   Ruby Lal, *Coming of Age in Nineteenth-Century India: The Girl-Child and the Art of Playfulness* (Cambridge, 2013), 5, 34.

73   Daniel Pick and Lyndal Roper, eds, *Dreams and History: The Interpretation of Dreams from Ancient Greece to Modern Psychoanalysis* (London, 2004), 4, 93, 97.

74 Robert L. Kagan, *Lucrecia's Dreams: Politics and Prophecy in Sixteenth-Century Spain* (Berkeley, 1990); Paul Edward Dutton, *The Politics of Dreaming in the Carolingian Empire* (Lincoln, 1994), 2, 26; Peter Dinzelbacher, *Vision und Visionsliteratur im Mittelalter* (Stuttgart, 1981), 136–40; Jean-Claude Schmitt, "Demons and the Emotions," in *Tears, Sighs and Laughter: Expressions of Emotions in the Middle Ages*, ed. Per Förnegård, Erika Kihlman, Mia Åkestam and Gunnel Engwall (Stockholm, 2017), 41–63.

4 Futures

1 Peter N. Stearns, "Shame, and a Challenge for Emotions History," *Emotion Review* 8/3 (2015): 197–206, at 197–8.
2 For example, Olivier Luminet and his colleagues at the Psychological Sciences Research Institute in Belgium invited one of the authors to present a paper to a group of psychologists and historians together in July 2015.
3 Paula M. Niedenthal and François Ric, *Psychology of Emotion*, 2nd edn (New York, 2017); Ad J. J. M. Vingerhoets and Lauren M. Bylsma, "The Riddle of Human Emotional Crying: A Challenge for Emotion Researchers," *Emotion Review* 8/3 (2016): 207–17, at 210, 211; Nagy, *Le don des larmes*; on crying in the Reformation, see Rosenwein, *Generations of Feeling*, 261–74.
4 Stearns, "Shame," 197.
5 Jan Plamper, "The History of Emotions: An Interview with William Reddy, Barbara Rosenwein, and Peter Stearns," *History and Theory* 49 (2010): 237–65, at 265, 249. Barbara H. Rosenwein, "Problems and Methods in the History of Emotions," *Passions in Context* 1/1 (2010): 1–33, at 24, online at http://www.passionsincontext.de/index.php/?id=557&L=1.
6 David J. Linden, *Touch: The Science of Hand, Heart, and Mind* (New York, 2015), 143; on separate neural circuits, see, for example, work done on the circuitry (involving both neuronal and non-neuronal cells) responsible for the sensory modality known as the itch and differing from the circuitry of pain in Dustin Green and Xinzhong Dong, "The Cell Biology of Acute Itch," *Journal of Cell Biology* (April 25, 2016): 155–61; for the interactions of circuitry, see Cyriel M. A. Pennartz, "Identification and Integration of Sensory Modalities: Neural Basis and Relation to Consciousness," *Consciousness and Cognition* 18 (2009): 718–39, at 718; Lisa Feldman Barrett, *How Emotions are Made: The Secret Life of the Brain* (Boston, 2017).

7 Jacques Le Goft, *Muei We Divide History into Periods?* trans. Malcom DeBevoise (New York, 2015 [orig. publ. in French, 2014]), 112.

8 Otto Brunner, Werner Conze, and Reinhart Koselleck, eds, *Geschichtliche Grundbegriffe. Historisches Lexikon zur politisch-sozialen Sprache in Deutschland*, 8 vols (Stuttgart, 1972–92); Stearns, "Shame," 202.

9 For EMMA (Les émotions au Moyen Âge), see https://emma. hypotheses.org; for Max Planck see https://www.mpib-berlin.mpg. de/en/research/history-of-emotions; for the Queen Mary center, see https://projects.history.qmul.ac.uk/emotions; for the Center for Excellence, see http://www.historyofemotions.org.au. In 2014, Palgrave Macmillan published the first books in its series "Palgrave Studies in the History of Emotions," edited by David Lemmings and William M. Reddy. Focused on the period 1100 to the present, ten books have thus far appeared. Around the same time, Oxford University Press launched two series, "Emotions in History," edited by Ute Frevert, and "Emotions of the Past," edited by Robert A. Kaster and David Konstan. the former is open to studies from the Middle Ages to the present, but so far has taken up only post-medieval topics. The latter investigates the history of emotions in premodern societies, including those of the Near East and Asia. Also in 2014, the University of Illinois Press began publishing a series called "History of Emotions," edited by Peter N. Stearns and Susan Matt. It welcomes books on a wide variety of time periods.

10 For the *New York Times* the word "emotions" was searched for the periods April 23–29, 1945 and 2017; for the *World Happiness Report*, see http://worldhappiness.report/ed/2017; for Google Ngram go to https://books.google.com/ngrams.

11 Maggie Berg and Barbara K. Seeber, *The Slow Professor: Challenging the Culture of Speed in the Academy* (Toronto, 2016).

12 Janan Cain, *The Way I Feel* (Seattle, Wash., 2000); Cherryl Kachenmeister, *On Monday When It Rained*, photos Tom Berthiaume (New York, 1989), 3–5. On the cross-cultural difficulties of interpreting smileys, see Ying-Ting Chuang and Yi-Ting Less, "The Impact of Glocalisation in Website Translation," in *Translation and Cross-Cultural Communication Studies in the Asia Pacific*, ed. Leong Ko and Ping Chen (Leiden, 2015), 239–60, at 232–7.

13 Cornelia Maude Spelman, *When I Feel Scared*, illustrated by Kathy Parkinson (The Way I Feel Books) (Morton Grove, IL, 2002).

14 Lori Lite, *Angry Octopus: A Relaxation Story*, illustrated by Max Stasyuk (Marietta, GA, 2011); Roger Hargreaves, *Mr. Happy* (Los Angeles, 1983).

15 Lynda Madison, *The Feelings Book: The Care and Keeping of Your Emotions* (Middleton, WI, 2013) in some ways offers a

position close to the one we are advocating. Pitched to girls 8–13 years old, and drawing largely on cognitive theory, it recognizes the possibilities of different simultaneous emotions of varying intensity. However, it is resolutely oblivious of social constructionism: "Remember that you're always in charge of what you do about the way you feel" (63).

16 Natalie Zemon Davis, *The Return of Martin Guerre* (Cambridge, MA, 1983), vii.

17 Amy Coplan, "Catching Characters' Emotions: Emotional Contagion Responses to Narrative Fiction Film," *Film Studies* 8 (2006): 26–38, at 26.

18 Dave Morris, "Introduction to this New Edition," in Andrew Rollings and Dave Morris, *Game Architecture and Design: A New Edition* (Indianapolis, 2004), 2; interview with Guillaume de Fondaumière, 2010, quoted in Jamie Russell, *Generation Xbox: How Video Games Invaded Hollywood* (Lewes, East Sussex, 2012), 244; Bernard Perron and Felix Schröter, "Introduction: Video Games, Cognition, Affect, and Emotion," in *Video Games and the Mind: Essays on Cognition, Affect and Emotion*, ed. Bernard Perron and Felix Schröter (Jefferson, NC, 2016), 1–11, at 2, 4.

19 Steven Poole, *Trigger Happy: Videogames and the Entertainment Revolution* (New York, 2000), 225.

20 See http://www.nicolelazzaro.com/the4-keys-to-fun; Nicole Lazzaro, "Why We Play Games: Four Keys to More Emotion in Player Experiences" (2004), online at http://xeodesign.com/xeodesign_whyweplaygames.pdf. See Paul Ekman, *Emotions Revealed: Recognizing Faces and Feelings to Improve Communication and Emotional Life*, 2nd edn (New York, 2007). For Geslin, see http://erikges.com.

21 David Freeman, *Creating Emotion in Games: The Craft and Art of Emotioneering* (Indianapolis, 2003), 10; see also Freeman's many websites, e.g.: www.freemangames.com and www. beyondstructure.com.

22 Perron and Schröter, "Introduction," 4, 7–8; see also Bernard Perron, "A Cognitive Psychological Approach to Gameplay Emotions," *Proceedings of DiGRA 2005 Conference: Changing Views – Worlds in Play* (2005), 3, online at http://www. digra.org/digital-library/publications/a-cognitive-psychological-approach-to-gameplay-emotions; Katherine Isbister, *How Games Move Us: Emotion by Design* (Cambridge, MA, 2016), xviii.

23 Susanne Eichner, "Representing Childhood, Triggering Emotions: Child Characters in Video Games," in *Video Games and the Mind*, 174–88, at 175, 182; Grant Tavinor, "*Bioshock* and the Art of Rapture," *Philosophy and Literature* 33 (2009): 91–106, at 92, 98.

24 Robert Jackson, *Rhetoric, Boredom, Horror Choice and Propaganda* (Winchester, 2013), chap. 3.
25 Chris Suellentrop, "Inside the Making of 'BioShock' Series with Creator Ken Levine," online at http://www.rollingstone.com/culture/news/we-were-all-miserable-inside-bioshock-video-game-franchise-w439921 (emphasis ours).
26 Barrett, *How Emotions are Made*, 24.

Conclusion

1 Thomas Jefferson, *Letter to John Page* (December 25, 1762), in *The Letters of Thomas Jefferson*, The Avalon Project, Yale University, online at http://avalon.law.yale.edu/18th_century/let2.asp.
2 La Comtessa de Dia, "Fin joi me don'alegransa," in *Troubadour Poems from the South of France*, trans. William D. Paden and Frances Freeman Paden (Woodbridge, 2007), 111.
3 Rüdiger Schnell, *Haben Gefühle eine Geschichte? Aporien einer History of emotions*, 2 vols (Göttingen, 2015).
4 On concepts embedded in grammar, see George Lakoff, *Women, Fire, and Dangerous Things: What Categories Reveal about the Mind* (Chicago, 1987). On China, Curie Virág, "The Intelligence of Emotions? Debates over the Structure of Moral Life in Early China," in *Histoire intellectuelle des émotions*, 83–109, at 88, online at https://acrh.revues.org/6721. On Thomas Aquinas, Rosenwein, *Generations of Feeling*, 162. On continuities, Bynum, "Why All the Fuss about the Body?"

Selected Reading

Basics

Some key books in the field, most already mentioned in the notes, include Jan Plamper, *The History of Emotions: An Introduction*, trans. Keith Tribe (Oxford, 2015); Monique Scheer, "Are Emotions a Kind of Practice (and Is That What Makes Them Have a History)? A Bourdieuian Approach to Understanding Emotion," *History and Theory* 51 (2012): 193–220; Thomas Dixon, *From Passions to Emotions: The Creation of a Secular Psychological Category* (Cambridge, 2003); Barbara H. Rosenwein, "Worrying about Emotions in History," *American Historical Review* 107 (2002): 821–45; William M. Reddy, *The Navigation of Feeling: A Framework for the History of Emotions* (Cambridge, 2001); Gerd Althoff, "Empörung, Tränen, Zerknirschung. 'Emotionen' in der öffentlichen Kommunikation des Mittelalters," *Frühmittelalterliche Studien* 30 (1996): 60–79; Catherine A. Lutz, *Unnatural Emotions: Everyday Sentiments on a Micronesian Atoll and Their Challenge to Western Theory* (Chicago, 1988); Peter N. Stearns and Carol Z. Stearns, "Emotionology: Clarifying the History of Emotions and Emotional Standards," *American Historical Review* 90/4 (1985): 813–36.

Chapter 1   Science

Two important introductions are Paula M. Niedenthal and François Ric, *Psychology of Emotion*, 2nd edn (New York,

2017); Lisa Feldman Barrett, *How Emotions are Made: The Secret Life of the Brain* (Boston, 2017). Catharine Abell and Joel Smith, eds, *The Expression of Emotion: Philosophical, Psychological and Legal Perspectives* (Cambridge, 2016). Dacher Keltner, Daniel Cordaro, Alan Fridlund, and Jim Russel, *The Great Expressions Debate = Emotion Researcher* (2015), online at http://emotionresearcher.com/wp-content/uploads/2015/08/Final-PDFs-of-Facial-Expressions-Issue-August-2015.pdf.

For more on the sociology of emotions, see Jan E. Stets and Jonathan H. Turner, eds, *Handbook of the Sociology of Emotions*, 2 vols (New York, 2008, 2014). On the anthropology of emotions, see Catherine Lutz and Geoffrey M. White, "The Anthropology of Emotions," *Annual Review of Anthropology* 15 (1986): 405–36.

For more on emotional management and labor, see Alicia Grandey and James Diefendorff, eds, *Emotional Labor in the 21ˢᵗ Century: Diverse Perspectives on the Psychology of Emotion Regulation at Work* (New York, 2012).

Chapter 2   Approaches

For more introductions, see for the modern world, Susan Broomhall, ed., *Early Modern Emotions: An Introduction* (London, 2017); for history in general, Alessandro Arcangeli and Tiziana Plebani, eds, *Emozioni, passioni, sentimenti: per una possibile storia = Rivista Storica Italiana* 128/2 (2016): 472–715. For a very brief outline, taking up the history of selected emotions, see Ute Frevert, "The History of Emotions," in *Handbook of Emotions*, ed. Lisa Feldman Barrett, Michael Lewis, and Jeannette M. Haviland-Jones, 4th edn (New York, 2016), 49–65. For an overview by a professor of rhetoric, see Daniel M. Gross, *The Secret History of Emotion: From Aristotle's Rhetoric to Modern Brain Science* (Chicago, 2006).

For the history of emotions with a focus on the expressive human face, see Stephanie Downes and Stephanie Trigg, eds, *Facing Up to the History of Emotions = Postmedieval: A Journal of Medieval Cultural* Studies 8/1 (2017), online at http://link.springer.com/journal/41280/8/1/page/1.

For the history of theories of emotions, see Rob Boddice, *The Science of Sympathy: Morality, Evolution, and Victorian Civilization* (Champaign, 2016); Martin Pickavé and Lisa Shapiro, eds, *Emotion and Cognitive Life in Medieval and Early Modern Philosophy* (Oxford, 2012); Dominik Perler, *Transformationen der Gefühle: Philosophische Emotionstheorien 1270–1670* (Frankfurt am Main, 2011); Peter Goldie, ed., *The Oxford Handbook of Philosophy of Emotion* (Oxford, 2009); Keith Oatley, *Emotions: A Brief History* (Oxford, 2004); Henrik Lagerlund and Mikko Yrjösuuri, eds, *Emotions and Choice from Boethius to Descartes* (Dordrecht, 2002 [rpt. 2008]).

An example of pre-1980s approaches to past emotional life (rather than theory) is Jean Delumeau, *Sin and Fear: The Emergence of a Western Guilt Culture, 13th–18th Centuries*, trans. Eric Nicholson (New York, 1990 [orig. publ. in French, 1983]). Dissenting, quite unusually at the time, from the paradigms of Febvre, Huizinga, and Elias were Hans Medick and David Warren Sabean, eds, *Interest and Emotion: Essays on the Study of Family and Kinship* (Cambridge, 1984). Elias continues to exercise great sway: see David Lemmings and Ann Brooks, eds, *Emotions and Social Change: Historical and Sociological Perspectives* (New York, 2014).

On psychohistory, see Saul Friedländer, *History and Psychoanalysis: An Inquiry into the Possibilities and Limits of Psychohistory*, trans. Susan Suleiman (New York, 1978 [orig. publ. in German, 1975]).

For emotion words, see Kyra Giorgi, *Emotions, Language and Identity on the Margins of Europe* (London, 2014).

For the ways in which theories of emotions are embedded in their own historical contexts, see Frank Biess and Daniel M. Gross, eds, *Science and Emotions after 1945: A Transatlantic Perspective* (Chicago, 2014).

Critics of the performative approach have particularly objected to the idea of ritualized emotions. See Philippe Buc, *The Dangers of Ritual: Between Early Medieval Texts and Social Scientific Theory* (Princeton, 2001), who criticizes reading rituals in the sources, and Peter Dinzelbacher, *Warum weint der König?: Eine Kritik des mediävistischen Panritualismus* (Badenweiler, 2009), who objects to reducing emotional outbursts to performances.

On various topics, see:

On particular emotions:

anger: Barbara H. Rosenwein, ed., *Anger's Past: The Social Uses of an Emotion in the Middle Ages* (Ithaca, 1998).
compassion: Margrit Pernau, ed., *Feeling Communities = The Indian Economic and social History Review* 54/1 (2017).
disgust: Donald Lateiner and Dimos Spatharas, eds, *The Ancient Emotion of Disgust* (Oxford, 2016).
fear: Joanna Bourke, *Fear: A Cultural History* (Emeryville, CA, 2005).
happiness: Darrin M. McMahon, *Happiness: A History* (New York, 2006).
shame: Peter N. Stearns, *Shame: A Brief History* (Urbana, 2017).

In general:

Laura Kounine and Michael Ostling, eds, *Emotions in the History of Witchcraft* (London, 2016); Susan Broomhall and Sarah Finn, eds, *Violence and Emotions in Early Modern Europe* (London, 2016); Erika Kuijpers and Cornelis van der Haven, eds, *Battlefield Emotions 1500–1800: Practices, Experience, Imagination* (London, 2016); Stephanie Downes, Andrew Lynch, and Katrina O'Loughlin, eds, *Emotions and War: Medieval to Romantic Literature* (London, 2015).

Emotions and religion:

Alec Ryrie and Tom Schwanda, eds, *Puritanism and Emotion in the Early Modern World* (New York, 2016); Phyllis Mack, *Heart Religion in the British Enlightenment: Gender and Emotion in Early Methodism* (Cambridge, 2008).

In specific countries or regions:

Curie Virág, *The Emotions in Early Chinese Philosophy* (Oxford, 2017); Luisa Elena Delgado, Pura Fernández, and

Jo Labanyi, eds, *Engaging the Emotions in Spanish Culture and History* (Nashville, 2016).

In the ancient world:

Douglas Cairns and Damien Nelis, eds, *Emotions in the Classical World: Methods, Approaches and Directions* (Stuttgart, 2017); Ruth R. Caston and Robert A. Kaster, eds, *Hope, Joy, and Affection in the Classical World* (Oxford, 2016).

For a bibliography of works on the Middle Ages, see Valentina Atturo, *Emozioni medievali. Bibliografia degli studi 1941–2014 con un'appendice sulle risorse digitali* (Rome, 2015).

Chapter 3   Bodies

On laughter, see Georges Minois, *Histoire du rire et de la dérision* (Paris, 2000); Jacques LeGoff, "Laughter in the Middle Ages," in *A Cultural History of Humour: From Antiquity to the Present Day*, ed. Jan Bremmer and Herman Roodenburg (Cambridge, MA, 1997), 40–52.

For more on emotions as practice, see Bettina Hitzer and Monique Scheer, "Unholy Feelings: Questioning Evangelical Emotions in Wilhelmine Germany," *German History* 32/3 (2014): 371–92.

On affect theory, see Eve Kosofsky Sedgwick and Adam Frank, eds, *Shame and Its Sisters: A Silvan Tomkins Reader* (Durham, 1995); Ruth Leys, *The Ascent of Affect: Genealogy and Critique* (Chicago, 2017); Michael Champion, Raphaële Garrod, Yasmin Haskell, and Juanita Feros Ruys, "But Were They Talking about Emotions? Affectus, affectio, and the History of Emotions," *Rivista Storica Italiana* 128/2 (2016): 421–43.

For emotions and gender, see Lisa Perfetti, ed., *The Representation of Women's Emotions in Medieval and Early Modern Culture* (Gainesville, 2005).

For emotions and space, see Hollie L. S. Morgan, *Beds and Chambers in Late Medieval England: Readings, Representations and Realities* (York, 2017); Joseph Ben Prestel, *Emotional Cities: Debates on Urban Change in Berlin and Cairo, 1860–1910* (Oxford, 2017); on mental space, or emotional experimentation, see Erin William, *Reading Melancholy: Sadness and Selfhood in Renaissance England* (Oxford, 2016).

On finding emotional meanings in art, see Patrick Boucheron, *Conjurer la peur. Sienne, 1338. Essai sur la force politique des images* (Paris, 2013); Johanna Scheel, *Das altniederländische Stifterbild: Emotionsstrategien des Sehens und der Selbsterkenntnis* (Berlin, 2014); Martin Büchsel, "Die Grenzen der Historischen Emotionsforschung. Im Wirrwarr der Zeichen – oder: Was wissen wir von der kulturellen Konditionierung von Emotionen?" *Frühmittelalterliche Studien* 45/1 (2011): 143–68.

For emotions and material culture, see Stephanie Downes, Sally Holloway, and Sarah Randles, eds, *Feeling Things: Objects and Emotions in History* (Oxford, [forthcoming]).

Chapter 4   Futures

On interdisciplinarity, see Daniel M. Gross, *Uncomfortable Situations: Emotion between Science and the Humanities* (Chicago, 2017); Felicity Callard and Des Fitzgerald, *Rethinking Interdiscipinarity across the Social Sciences and Neurosciences* (Houndsmills, Basingstoke, Hampshire, 2015) and online at https://link.springer.com/book/10.1057%2F9781137407962.

On overcoming binaries in ancient Chinese culture, see Paolo Santangelo, "Emotions, a Social and Historical Phenomenon: Some Notes on the Chinese Case," in *Histoire intellectuelle des émotions, de l'Antiquité à nos jours*, ed. Damien Boquet and Piroska Nagy = *L'Atelier du centre de recherche historique* 16 (2016): 61–82, online at https://acrh.revues.org/7430.

For studies of emotions in film, see Torben Grodal, *Moving Pictures: A New Theory of Film Genres, Feelings and Cognition* (Oxford, 1997); Ed S. Tan, *Emotions and the Structure of Narrative Film: Film as an Emotion Machine* (Mahwah, NJ, 1996).

On videogames and emotions, see Sharon Y. Tettegah and Wenhao David Huang, eds, *Emotions, Technology, and Digital Games* (London, 2016); Roberto Dillon, *On the Way to Fun: An Emotion-Based Approach to Successful Game Design* (Natick, MA, 2010).

Illustration Credits

Index